To Cathy, Bob + Robert,
peace + all
best wishes

Emotional Elegance

by Bob Beverley

Bob Beverley

To Victor James McNeight

My first grandchild

contents table

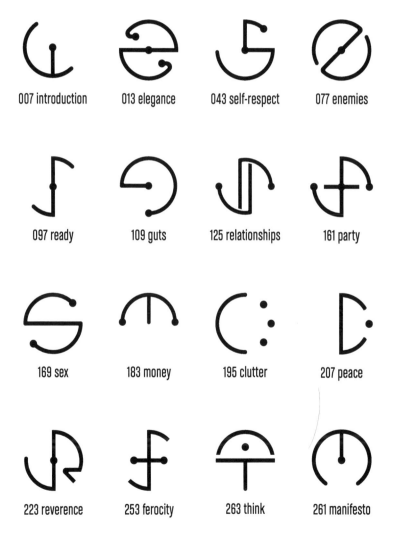

For most of my life, I've avoided seriously accepting, addressing and exploring the emotional realm. In my early youth, it was the source of almost unbearable disturbances. Dealing with that, I developed strategies of how to read and please people. Eventually I was able to expand my acknowledgement, expression, and tolerance for emotional stress and conflict, through several years of personal-growth trainings and experiences.

Nonetheless, in my early adulthood and career in productivity consulting and training, I experienced this arena of our feelings as mostly secondary to, and derivative of, how we think (mentally) and what we do (physically). Too often I noticed people using the excuse of their temporary emotional state as an excuse for not thinking and doing. How our mind focuses and the behaviors and practices in which we engage have great influence on how we feel (as well as our productivity).

In the last few years, however, I've gained a much deeper respect for the emotional aspect of our universe—our responses to it, the limitations it can produce, and the potential useful power inherent within it. We often become unproductive or highly so because of how we're feeling.

In the following pages Bob Beverley delivers an absorbing and comprehensive manifesto and manual for all this. On almost every page, I found myself saying, "Yeah, right, I could do that more, better, and more...elegantly!" It's agonizingly right-on and common sense, full of great advice, honest and heartfelt, and will undoubtedly touch you. It did me.

If you're reading this preface to decide if you want to read the book, don't hesitate. If you're reading it because it's just in the book, and you know you're interested...I'll stop now.

David Allen

Santa Barbara, California

A friend needlessly criticizes you and you say "That hurt my feelings." The friend says "I'm sorry, I took out my bad day on you, let's start over." You reply "I forgive you, tell me about your day."

This is emotional elegance in action--the ability to manage our emotions in a thoughtful, sophisticated way that leads to a better world for all concerned. You and I know this is not easy. In the above example, you could have pretended you were not hurt, stuffed your feelings, or responded with inappropriate anger. Or your friend could have felt so guilty when you mentioned your hurt feelings that he could blame you for being so sensitive. Or he could have been so offended that you didn't recognize that he was having a bad day, that he could have walked away and never spoken to you again.

Managing our feelings and our lives is a very difficult task, at times seemingly impossible. And the way we manage our lives directly affects how well we manage our feelings. What if you have a life filled with more than bad days?

It will quickly become obvious that the term "emotional elegance" is almost an oxymoron, especially if you listen to the dictionary definition of elegance: "Very choice, and hence, pleasing to good taste; characterized by grace, propriety, and refinement, and the absence of everything offensive; exciting admiration and approbation by symmetry, completeness, freedom from blemish, and the like; graceful; tasteful and highly attractive; as, elegant manners; elegant style of composition; an elegant speaker; an elegant structure."

None of us can come even close to "the absence of everything offensive" when it comes to our emotions, for they are too powerful, too unruly, and too messy. Think of rage, bitterness, lust, envy, sloth, fear, despair. These emotions are not easily subject to propriety, refinement and freedom from blemish. If you doubt me, read Shakespeare, the morning newspaper, or your heart the last time it was crushed.

Why use the term "emotional elegance" at all? I believe, first of all, that any of us can and must aim higher when it comes to the management of our emotions. The world needs emotional elegance, my term for a powerful, highly skilled way of living--a skill none of us can pull off perfectly, but one which is worthy of our lives. Secondly, I use the word "elegance" because it implies a link between emotions and the status of our surroundings and how we handle everything external in our lives. It is hard to be peaceful if we have no money, our house looks like a junkyard, and our spouse just walked out. In this sense, one could argue that I am an "emotional materialist" believing that our inner world is inextricably tied up with how things are going in our outer world. If you live poorly in most areas of your life, it will be difficult for you to be content, no matter how much you go to therapy or how much Prozac you take.

Emotional elegance is predicated on the notion that we need to be athletes in the emotional arena and that our happiness, our peace and our well-being are dependent upon most of the things in our life being the way we want them to be. The more elegant our life is, the closer it is to our ideal, the happier we can be. Emotional elegance is, of course, a very personal matter, and the way you want to live may be different from how I want to live--but, in general, most people are not going to be happy in a war zone.

If all this is true, our emotional well-being is very dependent on justice being a reality in our lives. We must recognize this fact, or we will easily blame the victims of violence, poverty, sexual abuse, horrific marriages, and brutal childhoods for not healing totally or for not healing faster. Our emotions are deeply bound to how we are, and have been, treated. If we do not believe that people are shaped by their upbringing and their surroundings, we'll keep telling them to "just move on" and "just let go" and "just get over it." And we will be oblivious to our own history, our own brokenness, our own need for a better life. Justice and understanding are prerequisites for any shot at emotional elegance.

Emotional elegance also requires humility, openness to feedback, hard work, practice and guidance. I would like you to view this book as your guide, as if you are having a series of long walks with me, an experienced psychotherapist, and we are conversing about all kinds of things. Listen for what you really need to hear, pick and choose what to focus on (as we always do in conversation), and, above all, live in a more elegant way, emotional and otherwise, for this is what we all truly need and deserve. I've given you lots to think about, lots to do, but it is your response that will make all the difference in your life.

To your elegance,

Bob Beverley

chapter one elegance

| ## elegance one

We all have what I will call an emotional elegance thermostat that sets an internal level of what we will or will not tolerate. Our past shapes the level of elegance at which we live--whether that be how much we suffer at the hands of others, the quality of our clothes, whether we eat a nutritious meal or one that is making us quietly sick.

The power of this thermostat cannot be overstated.

How elegant and delightful when...

A simple request is simply taken care of.

No passive aggressive hassle.

No complaining while the request is taken care of.

No needless delay.

Request granted.

A thing of beauty.

elegance three

How elegant and surprising when....

"I'm sorry" is said before anything else, when the person is truly in the wrong.

How elegant and smart when...

Someone stops the argument before all hell breaks loose.

018 elegance five

How elegant and right when...

An old man's story is heard in full.

elegance six

How elegant and dignified when...

We spot the beauty of an older woman.

020 | elegance seven

How elegant and soothing when...

We are heard and understood.

elegance **eight**

How elegant and wise when...

You know who your friends are.

elegance nine

How elegant and satisfying when...

You try to guide someone away from trouble with firm advice, and they listen to you.

elegance ten

How elegant and fitting and right when...

Your tears and rage let you know that you matter.

024 | elegance eleven

How elegant and right when...

You see the tears and rage of another person and you realize that they matter too.

elegance **twelve**

How elegant and apt when...

Blame is accurately and fairly given.

elegance thirteen

How elegant and uplifting when...

We do the one thing that really takes a load off our back.

Someone apologizes.

A room is straightened up.

An overdue bill is finally paid.

elegance fourteen

How elegant and perfect when...

You fix something as soon as it needs fixing.

elegance **fifteen**

Elegance requires one big Yes--and that Yes leads to practice and enthusiasm and growing passion towards the thing or person or project we love.

"It is in self-limitation that a master first shows himself." - Goethe

Elegance also requires that we use the word NO more often. Elegance requires limits. If there is no limit to our attention, our purchases, our eating, our interests, we grow tired and overwhelmed (the most common and powerful enemies to our psychic health.)

We rebel against limitations because we are grandiose and proud--we think we can be all and do all.

We are afraid of limitations because it is terrifying to be an individual, to make decisions, to say no to expectations. And so we go along with already set obligations and expected ways of doing things. We do not like to ruffle feathers, especially if we have never ruffled feathers before.

elegance **seventeen**

Human beings are satisfied when things are right and just, when things go the way they should go, when we function the way we should. We are not built to take much mess, whether it's bickering or clutter or a bounced check. We are not built to make much mess, because we feel guilty about the mess we make--the hurt feelings, the lost time, the buried treasures we cannot find because we have accumulated too many things.

No one thing can make us altogether happy. And things alone do not make us happy. What makes us happy is fixing our lives, getting more of it right, and enjoying it more.

We are also built to hunger and thirst after greatness, whatever that greatness may be. We are built to have passion, enthusiasm, and wild dreams--about matters that mean something, like making the world a better place. Mediocrity is not elegant.

elegance **eighteen**

Emotional elegance, as with any sort of elegance, is also about the cumulative effect of small things. It is astonishing to think how much emotional misery or delight is caused by simple actions, simple words, and a mood or two.

| # elegance nineteen

A lot of life is draining. Not elegant, not elegant at all. We can feel defeated and succumb to despair.

What can we do when we feel this way? It is tempting to stay home, do nothing and bury our art in a pillow, whatever our art may be. A more elegant solution is to be like God, to be a creator. You must create and receive great beauty, great truth, great love, great kindness. Such greatness comes in all manner of ways. You can reach out to a neighbor and tell them in no uncertain terms that their art matters. You can head to your piano or writing desk or knitting den and make some light for the world to see. If you are tired, you can go to bed and love yourself in whatever ways you do, and if you find anyone else in your bed love them too, for maybe no one else in the whole wide world sees them and loves them.

elegance **twenty**

Emotional elegance requires the ability to see when we are right to oppose the conditions in our lives.

"I do not like how you talk down to me."

"You do not pay me enough."

"I don't like the furniture in our bedroom."

If you take care of yourself, physically, nutritionally and emotionally, and if you live in happiness, it is easier for me to do the same. This is taking the buddy system to the max. Why does this work? We are social creatures, geared for family and groups. We affect one another. The light in you will light a path for me. If you give up, I am more likely to stumble.

Is this not a good reason to join a crusade toward elegance?

If you are going to compare yourself with other people, be grateful and inspired by the excellence in someone else and offer sympathy and a helping hand where they are weak. This is the grace of great living.

| elegance **twenty-three**

It is easy to give up, excusing ourselves because others appear better. And yet, still, someone precious is looking up to us, that someone's precious life is being shaped by us--there is no more elegant a thought.

Remember the times you have watched a movie or listened to some great music and your soul was stirred and you wanted to be more than you are? You wanted to be as strong and as alive as the hero on the screen or as powerful a person as the soaring music made you feel you could be. Remember how you felt when you knew that someone special really loved you and you felt it would be easy to love yourself and make every part of your life the way you desire it to be?

In those moments we see that we could be more "on fire." In those possibility moments we see ourselves at our best. We see the masterpiece we can be.

Possibility is stunningly powerful.

elegance twenty-five

The beauty of you is easier to see than you think.

Take in compliments. Believe those who love you when they tell you how lovely you are and in what specific ways.

| ## elegance twenty-seven

I imagine you have someone in your life who can't wait for you to get rid of something that has been dragging you down for years. They long for your release from captivity. They see your worth and know this something is not worthy of you. They yearn for the richness you deserve. Maybe we should gather our friends in a circle and have a yearning party where we get to hear what others are longing for on our behalf, and we for them.

A yearning party.

A longing party.

A festival of desire and belief, a chorus of resounding No's, a symphonic Yes.

Your life can be a work of art. It's high time for your masterpiece, is it not?

chapter two self-respect

| ## self-respect **one**

According to the Dictionary, self-respect is "a proper sense of one's own dignity and integrity." The path to self-respect goes through the drama of our lives and the murkier drama in our brains as we judge ourselves, question ourselves and assess the damages and the triumphs. What if you don't have total integrity? What if you know a few things about yourself that are not very dignified? Who doesn't?

Perhaps true self-respect rests on grace, humility, forgiveness and kind understanding--virtues not usually associated with self-respect. Self-respect is not a game of perfect.

What if you have been taught to demean yourself? What if you have learned to see yourself through the eyes of a never-satisfied perfectionist, a disapproving judge, or a mean tyrant? What if your mother was silent and withholding? What if your father hit you or abandoned you?

This screws you up.

The life you have is the product of countless internalizations. You have taken in a language, a whole world of beliefs and values, the felt truth of experience, all resulting from the "teachings" that have shaped your view of yourself and others. This internalization is so powerful because you did not even know it was happening. Do you remember learning English? Do you recall the moment the penny dropped and you felt either inferior or superior to others? When did you decide to join the cult that shaped you?

If you want your life to be different, be alert to the different vitalities that are now coming your way. Take in the praise, feel the delight of those who see your beauty, cherish the moment when you made a difference, hold on to the alive feelings when they overtake you, and seize the possibilities, the differences, the fresh look, the surprises, the creative spin on things.

You must leave home.

Now is the time for a new awareness. It is the time to abort the old filters that were set in place by the cults we grew up in. Someone may want to give you a slice of heaven: hear them. Let it in. Take it. And if someone runs at you with the negative or inelegant, erect new filters to protect yourself, rather than taking in the pain as gospel.

You need a new community to help you see who you are, compared to what you have been taught.

Self-respect is an evolving, ongoing reality. Everybody is a work in progress. However, notice the word "work" in work in progress. We grow in self-respect as we fix our lives.

self-respect **four**

I recently had a conversation with a man who is one of the top speaking trainers in the world. He is very successful and he told me that he struggled with guilt in terms of not deserving all that had come his way. I told him this true story about a cousin of mine whose husband is a gardener for one of the wealthiest families in the world. Their boss offered to let them live in a million dollar home in Westchester County and my cousin conveyed to me her discomfort with accepting such a gift. I asked her, "How do you sit with the fact that life has given you two sons, whom I imagine are priceless to you, worth far more than a fine home an hour north of New York City?" The cousin got my point as did the speaker. To paraphrase Jesus: we strain at pennies and have already swallowed diamonds.

self-respect **five**

Your life impacts the people who are precious to you. Your competence, your gifts, your presence can make all the difference in the world to them. Ponder this and your life should feel more valuable, more important, and more vital.

However, familiarity dulls our senses.

We try to look our best for the boss and look our worst around our spouse. We clean up the house when guests come over and leave it slovenly for ourselves. We save our angry words for the ones we live with. The people who are precious to us deserve our best self. We should live with self-respect around them and for them.

| ## self-respect six

Self-respect is sadly often automatically tied up with the cultural preoccupation with talent, success, wealth, and fame.

There is something in us that respects those who overcome adversity, put in the effort, and continually find their growing edge, even though they might never be famous, wealthy or the top star.

It will bring important clarity to your life if you know who you idolize and how you compare yourself to those you admire. Our minds seem to use comparisons in a way that is almost always destructive. We compare upwards and then feel bad about ourselves.

Want to compare? Compare yourself now with the better you that you want to be. Be sheltered in the arms of the ideal self you are creating.

| ## self-respect eight

I think we unwittingly and unconsciously fight against impossible ideals. Can we actually do all that we think we should do this week? Can anyone read all that we think we should in our lifetime?

We should keep striving toward our dreams. Yet, if you keep your expectations to a sane, manageable level, along the journey, you will have more self-respect, I promise.

Every night, take time to review the day. Be proud of the good you did. The extra kindness where you went out of your way. Money sent to help a relative. The timely bit of tact. Harsh words not spoken. The bad you avoided, even if it was a close call. Self-control. Whew! Be grateful.

Think of all the good you have done over the long haul--all those meals made, all the poems written while fear was yelling "Insignificant!" in your ear, all the miles driven to work, to bring home the paycheck to feed your family.

This review is an under-rated and vastly under-utilized path to self-respect.

self-respect ten

Yes, "through many dangers, toils and snares I have already come, Tis grace hath brought us safe thus far, and grace will lead us home." But you cooperated with grace. You fought, you hung in there, you overcame the bullies and the jeers, the silence of the uncaring. You kept going even though you were scared. You've won many a battle.

Think about it all. You are something.

Take time to review all the hurdles you have overcome.

Be proud.

Here is a series of quotations about self-respect and I intersperse my thoughts:

> *Self-respect is the fruit of discipline...*
> *~Abraham J. Heschel*

Yes, absolutely true—although I have never met a person who had total discipline or total integrity in their life. Perfection is impossible.

> *The willingness to accept responsi-bility for one's own life is the source from which self-respect springs.*
> *~Joan Didion*

If all we do is blame others for our flaws, we won't fix our lives.. Making our life the way we want it is the hard path to self-respect. Yes, others have hurt you and others can seriously get in your way. You can still own your life and fight to improve it.

> *To free us from the expectations of others, to give us back to ourselves - there lies the great, singular power of self-respect. ~Joan Didion*

With the reminder that self-respect is forever influenced by the others who have shaped us. Our expectations are formed by community after community. We decide, slowly, unconsciously, what to keep and what to discard. The expectations of others are inside us and we hear a chorus and then, eventually, sing our solo.

> *If you want to be respected by others the great thing is to respect yourself. Only by that, only by self-respect will you compel others to respect you. ~Fyodor Dostoyevsky*

However, thank God that there are people who respected us long before we had much semblance of self-respect or had a glimmer of our uniqueness and greatness.

> *Some people have so much respect for their superiors they have none left for themselves. ~Peter McArthur*

We all need our heroes, but save part of the pedestal for you. Indeed. Healthy egos are not intoxicated and they have room for others.

> *You punch me, I punch back. I do not believe it's good for ones self-respect to be a punching bag. ~Edward Koch*

It's easy to punch back when you are the Mayor and you have cops around you and money for lawyers. Nonetheless, listen to Koch--do not be a punching bag for anyone. It's not good for them or you.

> *Would that there were an award for people who come to understand the concept of enough. Good enough. Successful enough. Thin enough. Rich enough. Socially responsible enough. When you have self-respect, you have enough.* ~Gail Sheehy

Maybe. But our brains are hard-wired for "more, more, more" and greed is one of the powerful, attractive, deadly sins. When you have self-respect, hopefully you are less tempted by shiny objects. Maybe self-respect and wisdom are what lead to awareness of enough.

"Respect yourself and others will respect you." ~*Confucius*

If only that were true. If only it were that simple. You can respect yourself to high heaven and some hellish monster can lay you low in this here world. It's respect yourself, be shrewd, stand up for yourself, and carry a big stick--and you increase the odds that others will respect you. No guarantee, though. Jesus and Socrates and Jesse James were killed. They all had self-respect and Jesse had a gun.

It's a grim world, in many ways, which is why I so admire good people and know they so deserve self-respect.

"Self-respect cannot be hunted. It cannot be purchased. It is never for sale. It cannot be fabricated out of public relations. It comes to us when we are alone, in quiet moments, in quiet places, when we suddenly realize that, knowing the good, we have done it; knowing the beautiful, we have served it; knowing the truth we have spoken it." ~Whitney Griswold

"When we are alone, in quiet moments, in quiet places" is the opposite of going through our days at 126 miles per hour, not ever slowing down enough to know if we won the Grand Prix. Self-respect requires a mulling over in our minds, the remembering of a thousand triumphs, acknowledging that we are "in the game" and not going to quit, bloody though we be. We take the time to see our self, our life, our talent, our effort, our good will--and we take delight in our accomplished self. Self-respect takes quiet time.

The above is truly only known when exercised.

| ## self-respect fourteen

Does the person who helps you have to look down at you in order to help you? Do we always need to be helped by people we look up to?

Can't we be helped at eye level with full awareness that our helper is our equal in life's struggle, perhaps a few steps ahead in understanding, experience, wisdom—yet he or she still struggles? Who could turn around at any time and need help from us?

Our lives evolve through diverse and powerful processes that, you may have noticed, are not totally in our control. Recall the power and wildness of adolescence, the first time you fell in love, or the reeling aftershocks from a betrayal. The soul's reaction has a life of its own.

I remember standing innocently in my kitchen about fifteen years ago. I was thinking about nothing deep or important, minding my own business. I was already through my first round of therapy, seven deep years, and I had grieved a lot of stuff. All of a sudden as I walked from the kitchen to the hallway, I started sobbing like a four year old about the death of my mother and how much I loved her. I mean sobbing--heart wrenching, snot dripping, shoulders shaking sobbing, unlike I had ever done before. No rational, self-controlled, everything's cool, male in sight. And my mother had died at least twenty years before this cataclysmic moment that overtook a former philosophy major who could distance himself from everything!

self-respect sixteen

If your voice was ignored when you were a kid, it is quite possible you learned to ignore your wishes and wants and viewpoints. It is easy to "just go along" when the prevailing forces don't listen to you. You learn to please others and drift with the consensus, and then you can drift away from your own wishes and desires. And I want to warn us all that drifting and passivity and lethargy can cast a spell over our hours and days and decades.

It may not seem like a big deal, but having the courage to own your guts and brains in the operations and decisions of each day is an essential achievement.

Watch for the drifting state. It is often preceded by tiredness, a sense of failure or despair, and too much food and alcohol. It is often followed by surfing the Internet or aimless watching of television. The drifting state leaves a bad taste in the mouth, a numbing sense of waste.

There are tools and systems and ideas that can help us avoid this waste. Here are a few:

A pen to capture your plans, your dreams--whether those be small or big.

A list of easy things to do, or a great movie at the ready, for those times when you are starting to drift.

A walk, whenever possible.

A nap, deliberate idle time, resting your eyes, meditation, a prayer.

Vigorous exercise.

Music that stirs your soul.

Bed before midnight.

Friends who really hear you and believe in your voice.

A sense that now is always the moment to live with decisiveness and personal power.

If you grew up in the kind of home they write books about, you learned to wait. You waited in deprivation, guilt, misery and a pain that soaks to the bone. You can get so used to this pain that you do not even notice it. It is the air you breathe. It is normal. You sit there. It's not like you wait for it to get better, you just wait. And so people who grow up in that kind of home are experts at delaying their recovery. They are too patient. They can endure for days, weeks, months, years and decades what would drive someone else crazy in an hour.

What are you sitting with? What are you sitting in? What are you enduring?

If you have repeatedly screwed up something in your life, you also learn to wait in that misery, expecting things to be no different, hardly believing that they can be different.

Sometimes elegance is there when we take that shrewd, sharp turn in a different direction. We get sick of something and wipe our hands of some long-hauled misery.

Some things can be different. You don't have to always wait.

You wait in the foggy soup of procrastination, fear, and aimless generality. You do not feel very defined. You lack mission, blessing and purpose. You wait for an anointing, for direction, for a clearing. You wait for permission to be what you want to be, to do what you really want to do. The blessing, the purpose, the anointing-it always comes to others, the famous ones, the righteous ones, the always lucky ones, the strong ones. No big voice of permission drowns out your shame, your indecision, your vagueness. You wait in the silence of fear.

This is very painful, so you start moving. You do the usual things, busy things, obvious things, habitual things. You fit in. You look normal, but you are still waiting for a day you never expect will arrive. A day you become an individual filled with the blessing of confidence, the blessing of an unquestioned soul-filled purpose.

Alas, is this something we must give ourselves? How could it be that such powerful realities are dependent on us? How can you find power when foggy soup fills every inch of your soul?

This is not something we "just" give ourselves. It is most often given to us. Besides, even the most self-made man is not entirely self-made; we all need love.

"It may be the case that the deepest illness cannot be cured without a touch of heaven. There are miracles that occur in places hidden far from ordinary life. Therapy helps people find and believe in such places, so that, in time, heavenly, hellish, earthly selves become partners." (Michael Eigen, "Toxic Nourishment")

We must receive love. Loving people see your gifts, your innocence; they hear your voice, they honor the difference you alone can make. They honor your mission. Do you believe them? Can you believe them? It may be that only one person truly sees you and they may be seeing you for only a short while. How hard, how almost impossible, to believe that what they are saying could be the truth, and that the guilt inducing eighteen years of your childhood was nothing but bad luck; you were born on the wrong street, to the wrong people!

Heaven often comes only in a touch. Do not wait when you feel that touch, do not wait. Receive it. Cling to it. Believe.

Hateful, ignorant and apathetic people do not bother with you, as you play "Moonlight Sonata" or offer your own particular gifts. Sadistic perfectionists chop away at your talent. Self-centered people use your talent as a prop for their egos, or they pay no attention to you because they are the center of their world. And so you wait for the attention and the approval that never comes. And it never comes because these people generally get smaller and meaner and more unhappy. They get so small they have no room to see you.

This can go on for years.

And in those years you blame yourself, thinking that if you played the piano better, you would have gotten more attention, more approval. It takes decades to see the massive self-centeredness of the people who shaped you. You wait for the blind to see you, the deaf to hear you. You wait in a courtroom where you have always been found guilty. It would be wise to say "Run out of that courtroom" but the courtroom has been internalized and is now in your head!

Run from your own crazy head. Listen deeply to others, listen to the stranger who is not your father, your brother, or your old friend. Feel the truth from those who see you and love you afresh--take it in, take it in, take it in. Doubt the old standard view of you--it is so predictable, so worn, so tiring for you. Do not wait to hate your craziness. Be very angry at those who have harmed you, at those who have taught you to wait in dirt, those who taught you that you deserved dirt. They did you great harm when they taught you to wait forever for the gifts that should have been yours every day. The gift of seeing who you are. The gift of innocence until proven guilty. The gift of peace. The gift of your own voice.

You are very shaped by your past, and you must unearth its blessings, its pain, its sorrow, its abysmal folly, as well as the strength, treasure and talent contained therein. You cannot erase the past or yourself. But you can still head in a different direction. You can still change. You are not a fixed state. This is the magic of possibility.

The easiest way to be happy is to love another person and to seriously attempt to make their life magnificent, especially when they do not always cooperate. The easiest way to be unhappy, ironically, is to only love yourself. Self-centeredness backfires. That is one eye-opening truth. You have to see it to believe it.

Complaining can have within it the seeds of self-respect. You are complaining because you matter and you don't like your current situation. Complaining can be the beginning of your liberation.

Great complaining puts us to work on our problems.

The trouble occurs when complaining becomes such a habit that even when we could do something about our problems, or when people offer us help, we just go on complaining. This is a trap that catches many of us. And even if everyone within fifty miles is sick of our complaining, we do not seem to be aware of this "help-rejecting complaining" that is a real turn-off.

When life hurts us repeatedly, we can become powerless, victimized and habituated to our rotten luck. Fear may lurk beneath our complaining: we're not sure anything can fix our problem. We eventually feel that our only outlet is to complain.

We complain because it gets us attention--from ourselves and others. We complain because it gives us a bit of instant gratification--we feel sorry for ourselves and we are affirming our worth to be treated better by the world. And because we are caught in a trap of habitual behavior, it is easier to complain about our hurts and obstacles than it is to work and overcome them.

In this sense, complaining can become a hidden form of defeat.

If you suspect you are caught in this terrible circle, ask someone you trust to hold up a mirror to you. This may not be easy for you, but it is never easy to ask for candid feedback and break a self-destructive habit.

Shame deafens us in varying degrees to the rich, rich music of those who adore us. It keeps us from letting ourselves and our talents and our bodies be fully seen in the clear light of day. Shame is manifested in our slowness to put ourselves out there, in our inability to take in compliments, in always having the lights off when we make love, and in the quick, casual put-downs about ourselves or others that come from our shadowed selves. Shame is evident in the small, shabby and foolish moments that litter our day.

What can be done about this? It will come as no surprise that, at least in part, I recommend psychotherapy, so that you can listen to your history again and see the distortion in the solos and choruses of shame that came your way. But shame is so deep and so extensive that we also must make an all-out effort to live well.

Living well means many things. It is the opposite of folly—it is letting your light shine, it is seeing compliments as a sign of your divine dignity, it is relaxing in your bed and receiving love because you are worthy of such lavish magic, it is elevating others with your grand optimism for them, and it is cleaning up your office because you are no longer going to disrespect yourself by living in a mess.

We must live as royalty, not necessarily meaning that we need to own the Crown Jewels or amass the wealth of the Queen of England. But our words and actions must be dignified and elegant. We must live with reverence and care and sacred attention. We must live as if we matter—and the shame will diminish.

It takes such courage to do all this—because our shame still says, "Who do you think you are?" And it takes faith to do all this too—because shame's cousin, despair, tells us that we will never be different.

Love is a community endeavor. It takes a village to diminish our shame.

I imagine that you might have heard Jesus' parable about the Prodigal Son. It's the story of a young Jewish boy who asks his father for his inheritance (in itself, a shameful blow to the father) and goes off to a foreign country. He squanders all his fortune in wild living—so much so, that he ends up destitute and feeding pigs for a living. In essence, this is a story about shame, because the boy comes to his senses and heads home, in utter disgrace, hoping that the father will at least let him be a hired servant. He wishes for no more, knowing he deserves much less.

The father sees a different reality. When the boy comes up the driveway, the father doesn't see a fool or a shameful disgrace or a battered resume or a muddy bag of flaws. With utter ease, he sees his son—his dear precious son--who is home at last. He calls for a party and the best filet mignon and Dom Perignon champagne and a ring for his son's finger and a new robe and sandals for his feet and pretty soon the feast is under way and the pig's mud of shame on the boy looks like it is washed away by the enveloping wild love of the father.

If we were there, we would see the ring and the robe and the smile a mile wide on the father's face and we would share in the toast and the laughter and the simple miracle of a human being home and alive in all "his glory," even when that person thinks there is no glory to speak of. We would not be able to see inside the soul of the boy and so we would wonder how he feels and what he thinks. Can he take in such love and appreciate the vision that sees a precious son still intact and looks beyond (or maybe never sees) the bedraggled recent history? Can he feel the dignity that he never lost? Can he picture that what he feared his father would so assuredly feel was never for a moment in the father's mind?

And, of course, the far harder question is whether you and I can see that we have been the Prodigal guest at such a party and that there is a dignity to us that people are desperately trying to convey with their toasts and gifts and compliments and laughter and forgiveness and gratitude and adoration. Can we stand it that we are this loved? Can we stand it that our dignity is still so visible and that our shame is not the deepest and only truth about us? And can we welcome such love and bathe in its splendor-seeing honor? Or will we keep returning to the pig's mud in order to convince others that our shame is the deepest truth? And can we believe that there are those who would never stop looking for us to return to a dignity we will never lose?

| ## self-respect **twenty-five**

Albert Schweitzer once visited a wealthy woman who was interested in his mission work to Africa. She was showing him around her lush indoor garden when a big beautiful spider walked across their path. The lady went out of her way to step on the spider and killed it. Schweitzer said to her, "Can you make one of those?"

We all have our critics who step on us. And we step on ourselves. It's time for a point of view where not even spiders get stepped on. It's time where we all say to those who crush us: can you make one of me?

chapter three enemies

| ## enemies one

Can you name your enemies clearly and candidly? This is not easy because some of our most pernicious enemies are subtle and quiet. A lazy mood can overtake a whole evening. A harsh or unkind word can throw us off for a few days. Too much celebration can leave us sluggish. Comparisons can throw us into despair. And we can be so used to the feeling states that drag us down that we do not feel the waste of time, the loss of peace, or the diminishment of our power.

I think there is something in most of us that believes we are partially exempt from the damages that our enemies can do to us. It's like an alcoholic thinking he is not at risk if he goes to a wild party on New Year's Eve. It might be blindness, arrogance, grandiosity or wishful thinking or something else I can't quite put my finger on--but this illusion leaves us not totally defenseless, but certainly with a leak in the dam or a virus in the system. Is this what leads us to push limits, tempt fate, and stray just a bit?

Our grandiosity saves us from looking scared to others or being inwardly terrified. "It's no big deal" could be our motto as we slowly gain a few pounds, stop really talking to our partners, and slip quietly into debt. Maybe the sneakiest enemy is the slowest one, the one we under-estimate until it is too late.

| ## enemies **three**

We get so used to the things in our lives that hurt us, the people who diminish our well-being. And so we put up with the hurt another day, another week, another month, and all this so easily turns into years. We make excuses, we explain, we draw a line in the sand for a future day, we get angry and vent to a friend, and then the moment passes and we calm down. A nice breeze stirs up the sand and our line disappears, as does our anger, and forgiveness and hope fills us once again. "They are not so bad." We feel grateful.

This is not all horrible. If we left everyone who hurt us, we'd all be divorced twenty times over and we would have no friends. Emotional elegance includes perspective and graciousness. The enemy is the lowering of our standards, the inability to speak up at the moment and draw a line in the sand now. The enemy is our blindness to the passing of time and the missed opportunity to base our relationships on self-respect.

The system we are in can seriously hurt us. If everyone around you is exactly like you, who can ever spot how you are screwing up? If people near you have your same interests and passions, who will enthusiastically point out something fresh and exuberant for you? If no one in your circle is very brave, how can you learn to leap? If all your friends are drunks, who will stand up for the beauty of soberness?

The people of AA are right--it's the "people, places and things" that will either trigger a setback or foster necessary, long over-due growth. You, too, are very shaped by your surroundings. It's the way it is, the way we are.

enemies five

We all want someone to come and rescue us. Perhaps you are in serious trouble about something. Imagine, for clarity's sake, that your enemy is keeping all saviors away. You are going to have to rescue yourself this month, this week, this day, this very hour. What would you do?

If you don't do something, what is stopping you?

enemies six

The under-rated enemy of the psyche is tiredness. We humans are machines, in a way, and a tired machine is a tired machine. It's that simple, that complex.

enemies **seven**

Bad luck is one of our big enemies. In this age of scurrilous blame and fast, ignorant judgments, very few notice the huge place of bad luck in terms of success and well-being. And when any of us are sitting pretty, it is very easy to spout off about how everything is wonderful and going according to God's plan. We then forget the dire situations that are all around us.

> *"Before you diagnose yourself with depression or low self-esteem, first make sure that you are not, in fact, just surrounded by assholes."*
> *--William Gibson*

Human beings are very capable of being nasty.

Abuse is not a "feeling" problem in the abuser; it's a thinking problem--the abuser always thinks he is right. The abuser is very convinced about his convictions. He's right, you're wrong!

If people have been nasty to you, chances are that you have gotten used to it and are not as alarmed as you should be. In this case, consider going out the back door and running as fast as you can to safety. Your elegant self needs and deserves the luxury of peace and safety.

| ## enemies nine

We wait for a big voice to warn us about the error of our ways. We wait for a big voice to give us direction and permission. What if the big voice is mainly silent and speaks only in extremis, when it is almost too late? Why take such a risk? Why not listen to the quiet voice that is warning us right now about something, that is already calling us to where we really want to go?

enemies ten

We need lots of help. It is a serious mistake to think otherwise. In fear of looking weak, we look to ourselves for all the answers and become more at risk. In humility and courage, we reach out for help and our world becomes more secure.

enemies eleven

Waiting in silence and patience for injustice to stop on its own is very over-rated. The unjust are usually blind and very slow to change. Waiting plays into their hands.

enemies **twelve**

Eat right and your body will reward you. Eat bad stuff and you will feel worse, eventually, even though onion rings may be your hearty wish. (Just because I write this, does not mean that I am not tempted.)

| enemies **thirteen**

Sanity means seeing the otherness and separate reality of things outside us. In my opinion, we are not "one" with all things. Perhaps we should be in awe of any Higher Power that runs the universe. Perhaps that Higher Power is not our bell boy. Perhaps we can't screw with Mother Nature like we do. Perhaps we had better understand who we are dealing with before we yell at a neighbor or punch a bully.

I try to be very kind to whoever comes my way. However, I would never release a sociopath from prison or allow a pedophile to remain a priest. We can't control everything, but we don't have to be liberally silly and kindly stupid.

"The ruined man does not praise ruin." --Leonard Cohen

In our world a lot of foolish people seem to get away with their wild and crazy ways. Think reality television. Think Wall Street. And think of the sneaky, little voice inside you that keeps insisting that whatever you are sneaking around about is not going to get you. The people who warn you and caution you are just repressed--they don't know how to have a good time.

If you don't believe in being more cautious, read the newspaper or go spend a day at city court. Caution and you will become fast friends.

We all have the sneaky, "I'll get away with it" voice inside us. We also have the voice of caution. How has that voice cautioned you? What warnings have you been given?

Are you listening?

I have seen countless people, whose lives are besieged by misery, imagine that medication alone will make their life better. It seems that a lot of psychiatrists and drug companies foster this illusion. Proper medication is often essential--but so are healthy food, finding and giving love, a decent home, a job, loyal friends, personal therapy and so on.

enemies seventeen

Some of us are too busy. We know it, or at least we have been told it enough times. Busyness is sometimes essential, but a non-stop busy life is speed-drifting. It does not lead to an elegant path. Poor health, exhaustion, rage, and bitterness can follow. We might easily take to "stimulants" (alcohol, drugs, porn) just to be able to feel something. This is not an elegant path, nor can it be a path to emotional elegance.

A while back I was as busy as all get out. My colleague, Arlin Roy, told me calmly that I was shaking hands with the Devil. I asked him what he meant exactly, because I think solutions are in the details. He said "If you are always responding, responding, responding to what is coming at you, you are taking no time to be individually creative and you will lose the ability to create."

Words have not been written that adequately convey the way in which we can all be quite absent from our own lives even though we look like we are really present. Our minds can tune out, disassociate, retreat from reality, and spin off in fantasy with no one noticing. While I'm speaking to you, my mind can be elsewhere and so can yours--and since people can be such bad listeners anyway, we may not realize that it's far worse than we think. Not only did I not really talk to you, not only did you not really listen, we both visited another planet while we were allegedly communicating.

chapter four ready

I've been thinking a lot about readiness as it relates to change, growth, peace, safety and risk.

The change that will next happen for you will be either the change that is forced down your throat (eg. someone steals your wallet, you will be making a lot of phone calls) or the change that you are ready for. Readiness is akin to openness, the opposite of self-righteousness and stubbornness. We grow when we are ready, where we are ready.

We have peace, and feel safe, when we know we are ready for what is coming. This good state of being is achieved by the steady habitual practice of readiness in attending to perpetual necessities. Anxiety is often a result of leaving too many things unattended to.

Life involves risks--some worth taking, some best avoided. A big risk we want to avoid is not being ready for what we truly need to hear or where we truly need to go.

Are you ready?

Have you heard of the group of people called "minimalists" who radically pare down their lives to a small amount of possessions? I recently read of someone who only owns forty things. What would it be like if you took a tour of your house and office and counted how many things you own? Would you be brave enough to count the things you have not touched or looked at in 10 years?

Would it pain your soul to know how many unread books grace your shelves, how many magazines are still waiting for a glance, and how your closets and attics hide the things you just had to have?

If we went through our stuff and had some sort of farewell to all the things that we no longer care for and will never care for, we would be more ready for the next conversation, obligation, book or celebration that comes our way. We only have so much energy and time with which to pay attention.

ready three

When I write or speak I yearn for people to be ready for what I have to say. I know the preparation and pain behind my words. I want to make an impact on other people.

Lately I have been trying hard to notice the gift that others are trying to give me. They in turn yearn for me to be ready for them. Will I treasure their hard won proficiency, their earnest book recommendation, the sacrifice behind their blog, and the overall sheer fact that their lives and their effort is as precious to them as my life and effort is to me?

My brother, James Beverley, has written a significant book on world religions. He gave me a copy. Where is it? Oh yes, it's upstairs in the spare bedroom quite unattended to by me. I will go upstairs and hold it to my chest and truly contemplate his gift to me, the gift of his stunning knowledge and expertise. The gift of decades of work. I will put it by my bedside and read it every night till I am finished. For me. For him.

We have a department in our brains that dismisses things at less than a moment's notice. It has to be this way or we would be even more paralyzed by options, information overload, and endless advertising.

And yet I worry about our dismissive capabilities. We dismiss advice, compliments, suggestions and feedback as if they are all going out of style. Especially if it comes from our significant others, perhaps the ones who knows us best.

Even our own souls try to speak to us. "Slow down" they say and we reply "Tomorrow" and tomorrow never comes. Our bodies ache and tell us that we need more water. We drink more wine. Our tears have something deep to say. We stifle our tears as unmanly or hysterical. We feel the need to help the world more, but that is dismissed by a mere glance at the pile on our desk.

I think we should always have pen and paper ready so that we can capture the hints and the tips that come our way. We should take time at the end of each week to see what gem we might have dismissed, because "missed" is the biggest part of dismissed.

You can be ready in this moment for the light that is coming your way. A line from a poem can pierce your soul. Books can come across your path that will enrich you with wisdom and cutting edge strategy. A brilliant friend can chart your course and make it clearer. A wise guru will point you to another guru who will lead you deeper and further along the journey. Your therapist can offer you light every week.

There is a lot coming at you. Are you ready to manage it, not just now, but a month from now, a year from now? Do you have a system ready to capture the line from the poem?

Has the treasured book been shoved aside by another book or the pile of magazines? Will you remember six months from now what your friend told you? Will you be on it? The CD set from the new guru arrived? Anybody listening? Your therapist paid you a world class compliment. Will it still be playing in your head a year from now?

This type of ready is world class and rare.

So, do you have a system ready to capture the light that comes your way? If you do not, you underestimate the enormous volume that is coming at you. And you overestimate our brain's ability for storage and retrieval. The brain can forget a thing in seven seconds ("What did that speaker say?") as it moves on to the next thing amidst the thousands of items it processes every second.

How do we create a proper system that has us ready for what comes our way? This is complex terrain, so I humbly offer these thoughts on developing a receptivity system:

1) If you see the vital importance of creating a system, your brain will come up with unique ideas that will fit your circumstance.

2) It takes time, guts and a heart to heart with yourself to know what your purpose and mission is. If you know your mission and are brave enough to pursue it, then lots of things will be automatically weeded out of your life distractions. If you are scared to know or to pursue your mission, then distractions are an easy place to hide.

3) Do you have files in a cabinet, certain bookshelves, places in your office or home, safety deposit boxes, and files on a computer that are clearly designated for your most important work? If everything is all jumbled together, it will all feel like a jumble. All things are not created equal. The diamonds of our life and work deserve and need a great setting.

4) Even though you might feel quite scattered and disorganized, you can attend to new and old things

with proper attention and care. You might have a pile of unopened mail on your dining room table, but today is a fresh start. New mail can be sorted when you get it; the unopened mail will be next, after whatever is most important, which could be in the unopened mail.

5) Life and mission and business are often about the unexpected and the interruptions. This is a very powerful bit of reality that our fantasy-filled minds like to ignore. An interruption can be the most important thing, something unexpected can be heaven sent. Readiness is crucial so we can be ready for the serendipitous and the emergency.

6) Ask professionals for help with receptivity. A computer expert, a therapist, an organizer, and an administrative assistant could all offer shrewd advice that would sharpen your game. Experts see things we do not see and they know shortcuts.

Our receptivity to any system will be shaped by our unconscious or conscious values, core beliefs and overall life purpose. If I am writing a book on jazz music in Harlem, I may ignore or dismiss a friend's recommendation to take up yoga. Likewise, the system will be very shaped by my personality and current ego state. If I am depressed, I might pay little attention to most things. If I am grandiose, I may try to gather everything under the sun, become overwhelmed and accomplish little.

Picture a glass, brimming to the top with water, ice, and slices of lemon. It is full and will not hold anything else. Imagine pouring more water into the glass. All you end up with is water all over the place.

I know that one of the things we are all up against is that we are like this glass of water. We are filled to the brim with the waters of our life and, in our saturation, we cannot be as open as we would like to further ideas and actions and examination of our feelings.

Openness requires emptying--sometimes of old things so we can let in the new, sometimes of good things so we can let in greater things, sometimes of many things so we can let in a precious few things. A simple thing like openness is not so simple--it requires a shifting, an end to some things in order that other things might begin. It requires non-defensive humility, decisiveness, prioritizing, and courage.

Are you empty enough? Are you open? Are you prepared? Are you ready?

Some days we need to sort ourselves out. It's not that we're massively depressed or painfully anxious or howling at the moon for some awful reason. No, there are days when we are, plainly and simply, out of sorts, only it is not a very plain and simple thing to figure out.

Sometimes it is even hard to notice that we are out of sorts, because it can be such a quiet happening (caused by an accumulation of unnoticed things). Out of sorts is usually the small blues noise in our souls.

What can you do about it?

You can talk to a good friend or have a discerning talk with yourself and free associate to everything that has been bothering you lately. Get it out in the open or write it down on paper—so you can see and hear all that has been getting you down.

And what could be getting to you?

You could simply be tired and need a nap or two.

You could have put off the simplest thing and it's bothering you.

There could be a mountain of matters that you have procrastinated about—and though you are used to the mountain of delay, it still casts a shadow over your life.

You could need a romp in the hay.

You might have a hangover.

You plainly and simply need to drink more water and eat more fiber and fruits and vegetables.

A few people may have slightly hurt your feelings, and it all adds up.

You may need to get out of your house more and see the world.

You may need a little more time alone, even if it's just to do the bills.

It may be bewildering, at this time, to think about your grand and wonderful dreams. They can seem ridiculous, even impossible. The truth is that when we are in the murk and fog it is not the time to think big. Until you sort yourself out, try to focus on a small thing that is right in front of you.

"Take good care of yourself" is the opposite of neglect. Neglect is the common fall-out from depression, abuse, and (actually) self-centered, overwhelmed parents. If your parents neglect you, if the world neglects you, it is numbingly easy to not pay attention to the details of your life as you wonder around vaguely in a rather empty, distant and ill-informed mind. Good care requires lots of talking for it is through words and the accompanying actions that we acquire skill, worth, and attention. Words fill us (silence is not always golden) and call us from ourselves to attend carefully to the precise demands of reality. The world we live in operates towards precision and we pay a price when we do not function with alertness and competence. If you doubt me, don't pay the IRS.

chapter five guts

If you don't know what you really want to do, then you will never notice that fear quietly takes your hand and walks you away from your dreams, your vital contributions, your courageously defined essence, your lean focus.

What do you really want to do?

guts two

Fear haunts us at such an imperceptible level that we don't even notice that we are not doing the thing we set out to do. And there are always so many other good and important things to do (truly there are) that we do not have to notice that fear has taken us off our desired path. And no one will know.

It takes courage to sit down with ourselves, then, and see the quiet fact that fear has knocked us off course, even though we can still point to the good and important things we have done. Yes, we've visited our relatives and sent some money off to a charity, but we still know that we are too scared to assemble our book of poems. Yes, we've taken the online course on overcoming fear and we've answered all emails, but we have not started looking for the new job.

Guts isn't seen only in a warrior's cry and charge at the enemy. It can be seen in those who take out a pen and a piece of paper and track what it is exactly they plan to do, come hell or high water, regardless of how they feel and how big the lump in the throat. Courage is not the absence of fear, it is the mastery of fear, including the fear of getting the things done that no one else is tracking.

guts three

There are things we are already doing that require courage and other admirable qualities. We've probably gotten so used to the things we do that we do not remember our fear when we first did them, or acknowledge the tenacity and love it takes to do them for a long period of time.

Recently, I invited my friend, Michael Milea, to be a guest expert at one of my Mastermind retreats at Mohonk Mountain House in New York State. Michael is a trained boxer and I asked him to share what it was like to take a punch and battle fear in the ring? He said: "A boxer who is being trained professionally is learning things step by step in a context of growing discipline and preparation. So any fear I experienced is nothing compared to (and then he pointed to me) Bob who has, because of his genetic bone disease, broken his leg when he was simply crossing the street."

We get so used to overcoming certain things that we don't even notice our particular courage.

I used to live in all kinds of fear and didn't even know it because I was so used to it. Fear was normal for me. I knew something was wrong, but I just figured there was something wrong with me--"I'm weak," "I'm too sensitive," "I'm a sinner"--and somehow I have to get my act together, before someone finds out.

If there is one thing I can tell you that I did that made all the difference in the world, it would be this: I got lots and lots of help. Now often the people who helped me did not know there was anything wrong with me. I would beat around the fear-filled bushes without letting them know and, just the very fact that "he talked to me" or "she paid attention to me" was enough to clear my head for a day or two. Sometimes people would come to me for help--and helping them gave me peace and purpose. And I would devour books, listen to lectures and sermons, take notes, and capture the lifelines of wisdom that were there for the taking. Above all, my friends were priceless to me, because we had the true communion (good food, laughs, soul-baring talk, and just the right amount of wine) that brings peace.

Eventually, I went to therapy and have never stopped going. The words and words and words of therapy (lots of mine initially, more from my therapist as time went on) gradually brought clarity to the fog in my mind.

You can see from all this that a fear reducing life is a long, step-by-step affair. We're all looking for love and that is what so much of the conversation is really, often secretly about. And so staying in your room all the time is not a good idea. If you want more guts, get lots of help.

| guts **five**

"Let your yes be yes and your no be no," said Jesus, and what that means is "Don't step on your own voice."

guts six

The people around you are observing you. They need you. You are a role model, in that each of us gives an example of how to conduct our lives. Understand this and you will more carefully consider the choices you make, the words you say, the things you do. Your integrity and influential status will give your more conviction, more guts.

guts seven

We know that people can be murderously certain and ignorantly decisive. It takes guts to know you might be mistaken. Tolerance and humility are civilizing agents--prerequisites for emotional elegance, prerequisites for world peace.

guts eight

Do not worry about whether you'll have the courage to face something down the road. Facing today's problems head on is the best preparation for our fears about tomorrow. Guts today equals greater guts tomorrow.

| ## guts nine

I imagine there is something you are scared to stop doing that has cost you time, energy, money and aggravation. You are scared to stop because that would be admitting that you were mistaken. You prefer instead to plough on as if everything is fine and you are not capable of egregious error. This is the "sunken cost fallacy" in action. Best to have the painful awareness that you are a mere mortal like the rest of us, prone to folly and blindness and stubborn waywardness; best to have the guts to correct your course before things get worse. Do it today because hidden shame and lower self-esteem are building in your soul and will also only get worse. It will feel so good to stop the bleeding.

We all bleed.

If you need more courage, think of all the people this very day who are standing up at an AA meeting and admitting that they have spent decades messing up their life with alcohol. Decades. If they can count the cost, you can too.

Where are you sinking?

Stop it. Stop it today.

I used to think that strong people were only of one type--the kind of strength seen in people who never seem to blink, who know that they are always right, who never give in. And then I went to therapy.

While in therapy, I spoke about my father who was strong in a rare, honorable way. He had severe rheumatoid arthritis and yet that agony never stopped him from kindness, responsibility, gratitude for his blessings and his unbelievable determination to make the best of his situation. He is my hero. However, my father had a stare that would put a German shepherd in its place, let alone a little boy like me. And so when I wanted my hair to be of a certain length when I was six or seven years of age, all my father had to do was stare and mention his wish that my hair be shorter and, presto, my hair cut would be what he wanted, despite my tears and inner fury. "That's the way a boy's hair should look!"

I told my therapist this latter story and mentioned my father's power. My therapist with great firmness and mocking irony said "Oh yeah, right, what a powerful man to be able to put a little boy in his place!" I asked "If that isn't powerful, what is it?" "It's weakness!" he bellowed.

My world shifted.

The strength to be open to another's perspective, the strength to blink, the guts to admit you are wrong, the courage to give in.

| ## guts eleven

I used to think that strong people were only of one type--the kind of strength seen in people who can fight and argue with seeming aplomb and apparent disregard for what the other person might be feeling. And then I became a therapist.

One year I had two violent male clients and as I listened to their stories of vengeance and mayhem I saw that they actually did not see the humanity of their opponents. I realized it took no more courage for them to be violent than it would take for me to yell at a lamp. A great deal of the time what looks like courage is merely an animal doing its thing or the thing (rage, revenge, hatred) doing the animal.

The nobly strong and truly courageous see the humanity of the other person.

Do you have the guts to ask your most trusted advisor and yourself: "What is my greatest gift?"

guts **twelve**

The truly miraculous people are the ones who make their lives better even when they feel the impossibility of change. To paraphrase Geneen Roth, they understand that their minds can play its usual "music," but they don't have to listen.

chapter six relationships

If someone's behavior is getting to you, either deal with it inwardly in a complete way by saying "I don't like it, but I am totally going to live with it, as I understand this is who they are" or deal with it outwardly via a conversation.

If you can't handle the behavior, it is best to speak about it sooner, because you will eventually either be severely passive-aggressive and deeply resentful or blow up like a volcano. I have witnessed the anger of people who have been repressed for decades and it is not a pretty sight.

As you confront people, examine your motives. If your motive is love and a wish for the betterment of the other person, be brave and stay centered on that reality. Love will help you not be swayed by their defensiveness, beside-the-point comments and possible counter-attack.

I think the most frequent way we let people down is that we put up with their mediocrity, nonsense or self-destructiveness for too long. It is, of course, very tricky to tell certain people their faults, and it is impossible to tell the eternally defensive and self-righteous people that they might be mistaken. (See Jonathan Franzen's novel "The Corrections" for its brilliance in this regard.) Nevertheless, one of love's crucial tasks is to wait for the right time to point out a more elegant way, and that time might be sooner rather than later.

Here are a few tips on timing:

Most people who give advice do jump in too quickly, before they know the situation or the chains that bind the other person.

Examine your life and see if any impatience stems from misery about your own current behavior or stuckness.

Spend 99% of the time fixing your own life, and this will keep you humble as you offer guidance or ask for better treatment.

Should parents, politicians, gurus, therapists, novelists, ministers and poets ever admit to foolishness, chaos and misery? Do we have to imagine that our guides have their act all together?

A few thoughts come to mind:

We need admissions of folly that will intricately and intimately warn us and guide us, with higher purposes in mind. We laud our AA brothers and sisters who tell their stories in order that someone else can find sobriety. This is not the same as a drunken story given for laughs. Do I have the guts and wisdom to show you my fallibility in order that you can learn from my mistakes?

The revelation of folly and the conversation about mistakes is an intimate matter. Timing is of the essence. Is the listener ready for the revelation? Does the speaker know where the listener is at? Does the speaker need to confess because he is looking for healing, absolution or praise? What is really going on?

We most need to hear where people have their act together, so we can believe in a better way. It is hard to live up to our ideals, but we need to see that getting closer to them is possible.

I love it when people hurt my feelings. Extreme, yes, but let me explain.

Initially I hate it. It hurts. But getting my feelings hurt, keeps me sane. The swift thrust of a senseless remark into my tender heart reminds me how vulnerable we all are to the unexpected injury. You will never find me saying "Don't Let It Get To You" or "You Must Want To Be Hurt" or "You Are So Sensitive." No, all those theories are spun by people who have not been hurt lately and forget how tender we all are, how easily bruised.

When I get hurt, I use it as a reminder to be kinder to others, especially those who have been stepped on so much. In response to the wound, I also vow to be better to myself--if the world is going to be unpleasant, why not increase our capacity for self-love? At first, my gut response to the person who hurt me is to retaliate--two eyes for one eye, five teeth for one tooth! Usually, I am aware enough to know that this will be a bloody mess, so I channel my anger into gratitude for those who do not hurt me and an eventual exploration of where the other person was coming from. And I ask the tough question: did I have any part in creating the painful moment?

This work is a reminder to me how hard it is to be a person of self-control, courage, strength and engagement. How easy to distance, retreat and give up on the world. The experience of pain and its traumatic effect is why I tell every client a thousand times a year "I know how hard this is!"

We are all extremely tender. It is the way we are built. Many people are also clueless and self-centered. It is the way it is. Consequently, we must be as harmless as doves, as wily as serpents. And we must welcome into our life all the love, affirmation and support that comes our way. Extremely tender people need extreme care.

"People will not always remember what you said. They will not always remember what you did. But they will always remember how you made them feel." --Maya Angelou

relationships **five**

It's tough out there. We can't always see clearly. Don't confuse your enemies with your friends. There are those who would throw you under a bus, and there are those who care for you, flawed though they be.

Don't confuse the two.

Notice that the word forgive is composed of *for* **and** *give*, which means that to forgive one's self or others is to be in a giving relationship with them or yourself.

Everybody in our church seemed to adore Harold Arbo. He was our minister when I was a teenager, quite some time ago. One day he mentioned to the congregation that he was thinking of leaving because no one seemed to appreciate what he was trying to accomplish. He said that he would hate to leave and that he would change his mind if enough people let him know that he was having an impact. In my adolescent blur I could not quite bring myself to go tell him that I thought he was a terrific minister--so fine a speaker, so full of contemporary ideas, so interested in me and my world--but I did not think he needed to hear from blurry me.

Everybody waited for somebody else to tell him what he needed to hear. One day not much later he announced that he was leaving us because our silence had been deafening. I think most everyone in church either visibly cried that day or cried in their hearts.

At his farewell party we finally made it clear what he meant to us.

Sometimes we don't feel like going out of our way for people. However, notice this: most of the time when you leave the birthday party, the home, the funeral, the wedding or the little get together after work, you are glad you did what you did. It was the right thing to do.

A friend and I were discussing a falling out that she had with mutual friends a long time ago. She told me one of the estranged friends had gotten very sick and had to be looked after extensively by his wife. My friend mentioned the details of their struggles and their heartache and then she paused, looked right at me and said "The trouble between us dissolved in the importance of things."

I literally gulped and sat silent as I let her wisdom sink into my being. I said something quite feeble in reply because all my energy was consumed in not forgetting what she had just said.

The importance of things. Perspective. Priorities. Reminders about what matters. The humanity of those who hurt us. Our humanity as we are hurt and, quite possibly, hurt back. But before all that, after all that, and bigger than all that--the importance of things.

In my therapy work and in my life, I see people playing with matches all the time. They do not seem to realize they are playing with fire.

A couple comes for therapy. They both have legitimate complaints about their partner. They both acknowledge its veracity. He admits he gets quarrelsome when he has had a few; she fesses up to taking him for granted in terms of romance. And yet both will persist in their behavior until all hell breaks loose and there is shouting, tears, and threats of a break-up. They played with matches and fire broke out. No surprise there, but they almost always look surprised, innocent, and bewildered.

"And often enough, when we think we are protecting ourselves, we are struggling against our rescuer."
--Marilynn Robinson

Your friend has a bad habit. Everyone you know lovingly warns him about big trouble ahead. He acknowledges the warnings and yet keeps on striking the match. It's the classic "I'll quit tomorrow." It is hard to stop doing something when all seems well today, when the trouble is distant. Eventually, everyone gives up and lets him be. However, when the flames start, the fire will not let him be.

How easy to give up too soon in warning others, especially, as Robinson says, when they struggle against us.

How easy to hold back our severe warnings, since we don't want to look judgmental, be offensive, or get scolded in response to our warning.

How easy to forget the real issue: matches are dangerous, fire is coming.

How easy to spot the match in another person's hand. What is that in your hand?

"No one likes me."

"I will always be the outsider."

"Everyone will laugh at my art."

"I am ugly, even though she said otherwise."

"I will never make it; things will always be the same."

The crazy thoughts and feelings roam in our brains. We are so used to them. They seem all powerful, as true as true can be. It feels like we can do nothing about them. We seriously and persistently doubt those who tell us otherwise, those who give us an alternative version. We don't even give it a second thought. We do a few things that make us crazier--like sitting alone in our craziness when we should be calling a friend, like drinking alcohol when our minds are already partly out to lunch. We play with the matches of our craziness. I have seen very few people in my day who are sufficiently mad at their craziness--OR DO ENOUGH ABOUT IT. We seem to think there is nothing much we can do about it--it will just go on and on.

The first important step is to understand that we can do a massive amount of fire prevention when it comes to our sanity. We can talk to friends, go for long, meditative walks, read books, go to therapy twice a week, and seek help to change any bad habit that exacerbates our particular mental ill. When I was studying to become a psychotherapist, my fellow students and I were required to go to therapy four times a week--two individual sessions, one group session, and one peer support group. It made us realize the enormous complexity of the human soul, the power of our hurts and crazy thoughts and feelings, and the vast array of equipment that is available for this most important fight.

"Women, some women anyway, do not enter marriage for a casual ride down the road. When they marry, it's their one big trip, especially if there are children, and if you stop and let them off, it takes something out of you to look back at your wife and your children by the side of the road and see that dazed look on their faces." --Gregory Hemingway, Papa: A Personal Memoir, p. 93

In my therapy work, I have seen the dazed, bewildered, enraged faces of those who have been left off by the side of the road. They hurt even more when they have been abandoned by someone who promised more, who pledged eternal love.

We are mature enough to know that some relationships are a bad mix and misery does not have to go on forever. Divorce is the funeral of a death that already happened. We know this, as we also know that some teenagers create hell, some friends turn out to be enemies, and there are places in the world where we should not stray.

However, there is a difference between fair and regretful dissolution of relationships and the nightmare that ensues when the pathologically self-centered repeatedly leave disaster in their wake.

We all are capable of immense self-centeredness and crazy moments where we could abandon anybody in our rage, self-pity, wild hurt, lust, drunkenness, or greed. Oh, the disasters we have avoided because sanity prevailed, we kept our mouths shut, nursed our wounds, kept our hands to ourselves, and thought about tomorrow, the bigger picture, and the reality of those in our care.

Judgments are a vital part of life. But if you want to have more peace, be less judgmental of others. The best we can hope for is probably this: judge less often, more slowly and more accurately. As we feel judgment building in our soul, we need to ask "Do I know the whole story?"

"How come you can see the speck in your brother's eye and cannot see the log in your own eye?" This means that most of our time should be spent fixing our own lives, judging ourselves as wanting in a certain area and doing something about it.

Your emotional life will be more elegant if you take the log out of your own eye. If you don't see the log, ask your partner or a truth-speaking friend or your teenager for help.

How can we be kinder to others?

1. Slow down, as often as you can. Hurry and lateness makes us anxious, guilty, pressured, and eventually meaner. None of this is easy, just obvious. Once you slow down enough to see it.

2. Truly understand that your background might have really hurt you deeply. It could be the same for other people too. It is more work than most imagine to recover from a difficult childhood. There is no quick fix. Trust me, I've looked all over the place for such a thing. It does not exist and thinking that it does is an egregious error that leads to impatience, tactless advice, and all manner of unkindness.

3. It takes energy to take a second look, hold your tongue, control your anger. Energy is the fuel of morality. It is far easier to be mean when you are tired.

4. We all fight (and are run by) fixed and very powerful realities. Instant gratification. Laziness. Food, food, food. Lies in the lust. Greed. Fear. Freud was right to talk about our drives. We are all driven people. Yes, we can do better. It is very hard to do better. Not just for you. Lord, have mercy on us all.

5. Pain is the great teacher. That's the way it is. We all have had to learn the hard way.

6. Softness, gentleness, consideration, understanding, forgiveness.....it feels way better than anything

promoted by a rap song. It works far better too.

7. It can take about ten years to know someone. Do not easily trust your simple, one-sided view of a person, especially if you are angry. Come to a conclusion after you settle down. Make permanent decisions when you are in a calm mood. An angry brain has a very low IQ.

8. It is difficult to be a child, a teenager, a young adult, middle-aged (when the comparisons really start to fly in your jealous brain and tiring body) and old. It is difficult to be a good father, a good mother, a wise son or wise daughter. The effort alone, for all of this, deserves great praise.

relationships **eighteen**

Be suspicious of the hard things, and very careful around them:

Hatred.

Resentment.

Bitterness.

Envy.

Sarcasm.

Hard drinking.

The hard worn path of your unnecessary suffering.

The hardness of being so used to your suffering that you trudge on as if nothing can make a difference.

Hard-heartedness is not as much fun as advertised and the hard things are more deadly than we realize.

I must warn you about splitting, just as my therapist warned me about this most primitive defense mechanism when I was first in therapy so many years ago. Splitting is where we make people or ourselves either all bad or all good. It is our reactionary tendency to demonize people when they hurt us. We then keep a rigid, steel-like grip on how bad they are and insist that any evidence to the contrary is a rare exception to their worthlessness.

There is something in us that feels grown-up or sophisticated when we act out, feel or live in hatred. If we've been unable to be assertive for many a year, it will be tempting to dabble in rage and revenge, if only in our hearts and inner dialogue. Hatred can feel so right, so grown-up; likewise, we can readily acknowledge that we deserve our envy and bitterness and resentments—we do have it tough, they do have it better!

Every hard-hearted thought and action comes with its own natural justifications, built-in defenses, and evolving "of course" reality. Our pathologies become one with our ego; our darkness will slowly be seen as light. To seal the deal, we will gradually and imperceptibly only hang around those who agree with us. The soft ones will be seen as sissies, as weaklings; the virtues will be viewed as bygone irrelevant notions worthy of a smirk. Change will be viewed as a very remote, unnecessary and quaint possibility.

If you want to know if you have slipped into hard heartedness, you will see a lack of tears, openness, laughter, compassion, forgiveness and fresh, new beginnings. The muscles in your face will feel tight and your eyes will be more focused as if danger is approaching. You will be short with people, easily irritated and exasperated by them. Nothing will much move you or touch you and you will just know "This is the way it is always going to be." If you start to feel anything deep or spiritual, you will just get busy with the usual things.

A moment's thought will make us see how understandable it is to be hard hearted and to flirt with the hard things. It is a defense against pain and loss and a natural reaction to the hard things of life that happen to us. If you were raised in brutality, we can expect you might have a chip on your shoulder and a rock in your heart. If you were raised in utter poverty of emotion, you might have few internal riches to share.

It is very easy not to notice our "small" hatreds and cold, little indifferences. What's the big deal if you have written off your mother-in-law when you compare it to a murder in the inner city? Who will be alarmed when middle aged people stop keeping up with friends out of a weary battle with unending obligations? Who will blame us for leaving our spouses or teenagers when we all know how hard it is to live together? In many ways, it is so easy to say "Enough is enough" and all the easier when we have lost a common, expected morality that fosters duty, patience, and utmost diligence about the sacredness of every person.

When my family cleaned out the house that I grew up in, I came across something that took my breath away. Amidst a pile of papers and old school books, on the table in the bedroom by the old brown lamp, I saw one of those small square tags that you put on Christmas presents. It had my little boy writing on it that read "To the best Mommy in the whole world. Love, Bobby."

The softness of a child.

The pure love of a little boy.

My mother had her flaws, but she was my mother and I loved her with all my heart.

A part of me does not want to admit that heart soaked truth.

"A rock feels no pain, and an island never cries."

Needed:

Many kind words. Occasional firm corrections given out of respect, not out of a bad mood.

Openness to feedback.

The humble effort to see others and our own self in all complexity.

Forgiveness.

Lots of comedies.

The hard worn path of our suffering makes most of us feel hard and defeated, perhaps numb. We hardly notice this condition because we are so used to it—it doesn't even feel like pain. And so we would never cry, as if our one heartbreakingly real life matters that much. No, we trudge on as if nothing can make a difference. We endure, we carry on—"I'm fine, thank you, no big deal, that's how it goes." Life teaches us to suffer and how to suffer. The hardness, the numbness, the usual sense of defeat. This is how it goes. It is not our fault. It is an essential part of the human condition. The hardness protects us.

We see someone else in their pain and, for a moment, we feel sorry for them. And then, oh so quickly, we forget about them and get back to our routines and worries and obligations and all that we have to do to keep our world together. This is how it goes. It is an essential part of the human condition. It protects us. And God knows we better protect ourselves because deep down we know and fear that not too many people have our back.

I propose something strange for you and me. It is so strange that it will be easy to keep on reading this to the end and then do nothing about it, because we are so busy with business as usual, our standard protocol. We won't want to appear different or be that different. We return to our stoical attitude and cool manner so we can handle the roughness of life. We'll take our character, our normal existence, ragged though it be. We live in a way that says "Do not disturb me very much." We all have our walls.

And we need those walls because we need protection from violence and meanness and stray bullets. We cannot take on the whole world and be an open book, an open wound, to all human suffering and need. We must have our limits. We are not God and, by the way, tell me, those of you who do believe in God, tell me how on earth does God ever sleep? If God loves us all, God must not have a moment's peace. If we are all children of God, then when God saw the picture of that crying little boy on the front cover of the New York Times the other day and knew that the little boy was crying because his father was killed by a sniper in Syria then maybe God cried and cried and cried because the father is God's child too and so is the sniper and...I am not sure how even God can handle all that.

Maybe God just cries all day long.

Jesus wept.

And this is what I am proposing for you and me. That we cry. Cry for yourself and your hard worn path of suffering. Give yourself the luxury of time and see how that path was formed, whatever it may be. See, just see, the folly and circumstance and dumb decisions that led you down that road. See, just see, the hardheartedness and stubbornness that has gotten you to this place. Maybe it was some other person's folly and hardheartedness. Maybe it was your own. It won't hurt you to give yourself understanding and sympathy and genuine regret. And out of that human warmth and kindness maybe you can start heading down another road and wouldn't that be nice and kind and smart and wonderful? You don't need to protect yourself anymore with your sarcasm and toughness and the hard pretense that you really like this old, weary way of living. Open up to total love of yourself in all its impossible glory. Give yourself a shot. The soft virgin road of your new beginning, even at your age. Do it and your tears will turn to laughter and your hardness to grace.

It's a start, heading down another road.

And take the time to figure out who you really care for and propose to yourself that from now on you will not give them the short shrift out of our very mistaken well paved road of mindless busyness. No, we must be brave and soft and loving and, in all sanity, in all sanity, remind ourselves that "all salvation is local" and that we must make time for one another in all our endless need for love and attention and care. So turn off your television and make yourself a local list of all the people you love, all the people you will cry over when their days are done—and list their birthdays and phone numbers and anniversaries and addresses and live as if they matter to you, because they do, because they do.

And time is not the issue. The issue is that we are crazy and we have our priorities all wrapped up in our hardhearted defensiveness against our own pain, against our own ability to love more, aligned with our wish to not be disturbed very much.

If you insist that time is the issue, listen to this story, a story (written with her permission) about a friend of mine who is kindhearted beyond compare. She thinks of others constantly and goes out of her way to do thoughtful things for her local cadre of hurting people. She has often not received such tender care in return and was lamenting her propensity to keep on giving to those who did not seem to notice her. She is sick of the situation.

This friend was in a horrific car accident years ago and she is on disability and has more time on her hands than most people. I told her that one of the explanations for her kindness is that she has more time on her hands, whereas others do not have as much time to think of others and do things for them. I informed her about the research done at Princeton Seminary where three groups of students were situated in three different rooms on campus. One group was instructed to simply chat with one another, another group was told to study a Bible passage that was rather innocuous, and the final group was asked to study the Good Samaritan parable—the famous parable about being kind to strangers in need. Each person in every group was then told to go separately to a different location and they were given various amounts of time to reach that location. Unbeknownst to each participant, along the way the researchers had planted various strangers who were in need of assistance. The researchers wanted to see whether it made any significant difference whether the student had read the Bible or the Good Samaritan parable in terms of help given to those in need. It turned out that the only significant factor that made any difference in terms of charity was the amount of time pressure that the student was feeling. The more time pressure, the less people stopped to help.

My friend pondered this story and later that night phoned me and said "I wonder what would have happened if money was strewn along the way."

And time is not the issue. The issue is that we are crazy and we have our priorities all wrapped up in our hardhearted defensiveness against our own pain, against our own ability to love more, aligned with our wish to not be disturbed very much.

"Be home for bath time. Kids grow up real fast." --David Hieatt

When my kids were young, my older friends gave me the same advice. I nodded "Yes, I know" as if I understood the passing of time, the necessity of rapt attention to the glory days of young children. It now seems that it all went way faster than I could have imagined. Be home for everything, be present to everything, it all goes by real fast--who can stay awake to that almost incomprehensible reality?

This bears repeating:

People are very tender inside. None of us can take very much emotional pain. This is a fact I would stake my life on. So speak tenderly most of the time and give out compliments like they are going out of style.

Consider the moment when someone talks to you and they really want you to listen. It is a tender, fragile moment. One heart to another, as a person quietly searches for the dignity of being attended to, softly asking "Do I matter?"

| relationships **twenty-nine**

How are you feeling right now? Anything bothering you that you might dump on someone else unwittingly or deliberately?

Some days I am tempted to think that we are here on this earth to say words to one another that let us know what a good job we're doing and how lovely we are. And some days I think that is purpose enough.

162 chapter seven party

party **one**

In the past ten years I have listened to a lot of marketing and persuasion advice. I have seldom heard any guru talk about how excessive eating and drinking hurts the sales process, the sales person or the person interested in productivity. Is there some conspiracy going on here? How many Mondays are written off because the sales person is in a complete fog? How long does it take for someone to recover completely from a hangover? At what point does the amount of food or drink turn into a shot of anesthesia?

How easy to forget that alcohol is a drug. How easy to go along with the crowd.

The three glasses of wine slip you into the land of conviviality and the carefree evening you feel you deserve. You are not drunk and you are far from entering the land of bulimia. However, this is just enough of a hit to the system that you will not finish your new book, or even go out and enjoy a good movie, and there is absolutely no chance that you will finish whatever chore you hate to do, because that is iffy even when you are in your best shape.

party **three**

Do we party just enough to harm our work and work just enough to harm our play?

I think we eat a bit too much and drink a bit too much and fiddle around a bit too much because it is scary to admit what we really want to do. It is scary to hold ourselves accountable to our dream. Or to acknowledge that we don't have a dream.

And, make no mistake, we can postpone our dream by doing all kinds of things that are of lesser importance to us, that are in and of themselves not harmful at all--we can fiddle around with chores, housework, phone calls, emails, and certain body parts, all because we dare not get naked with our unique vision and compelling dream. An all-encompassing assertiveness about everything we do may seem like we are taking ourselves a bit too seriously, or certainly the less-driven might think so: "Relax, dude, take a chill pill, it's only a few beers, the week is young."

I hardly ever hear anyone speak about how great it feels to be clear-headed, sober, fit, limber, not hungry, not full, yet eager for the delicious things of life. I hear a lot of people brag about their drinking exploits and carefree pot-induced evenings. What gives? It's not that I'm against people feeling good. It's just that I want to know what works the next day and in the long run and I find honest discourse very much missing about these things.

"Play is an expression of the dignity of the soul, enslaved to no bondage of justification." --Joanna Field

And what are the delicious things of life for you?

chapter eight sex

Loving sex can feel so elegant, so right, that a word or two must be said about it.

But who has the words? And who can do justice to the vast complexity of our powerful desires for love and ecstasy all mixed in with strange thoughts, endless compulsions, fear of rejection, self-centeredness, body shame, lack of desire and getting older? We all seem to judge so easily in this sphere, though it is very difficult to turn the mirror on ourselves.

We are built for love and ecstasy. There are a million nerves in your body, built for pleasure beyond compare. You know what I mean. Your heart still skips a beat at the memory of your first love. You know what I mean.

Every luscious body is inescapably linked to a tender soul and a life that is real. This is the central reality that lust ignores and the current "friends with benefits" culture glibly denies. Sex is always about people and people are more real than our self-centeredness likes to imagine.

The Golden Rule ("Do unto others...") can apply to dating, initiation of romance, and a lengthy relationship. In these situations, The Golden Rule means it's your move! You can ask the other person out. You can make the first move with your partner, if it has been a while. You can start the "I'm sorry" conversation and the forgiveness process. You can plan the wild night. Why not?

The "serve-me, I don't want to have to ask for anything, I want it to all to come to me" passive part of us will not like this advice. Loving sex is about giving and receiving. True giving and deep receiving is not passive. Love is an active affair.

| sex three

We all want to be adored. This seems to me to be at the heart of sexuality. Not a bad wish. We all are built to adore others. It is as blessed to adore as to be adored. It's not a bad idea to adore yourself, now and then.

Everyone I have ever met takes their partner for granted to some extent. It is the way things are, otherwise we would die of infatuation. Nevertheless, we can fight the trend of habituation. Sexual neglect is the common cold of long term relationships. Colds are lousy. Who wants to have a cold forever?

Nobody owns another person, emotionally or sexually, although some may try. If you doubt me, become a therapist and listen to the fury of the presumed to be previously owned who have been controlled, nagged at, stepped on, abused and very much taken for granted. If you think you can own someone, you are in for a lonely ride, whether you know it or not.

Greed is a very dangerous thing. "Count your blessings" works well in the sexual sphere too. Wrecking your life for most anything is not worth it. Think long term when it comes to your actions.

What will you feel like in the morning?

Will you be happy nine months from now?

If I say to you "Be careful," what comes to mind?

A loving sex life requires courage--the courage to believe in yourself, to go for more, to open up to another and trust; the courage to choose wisely; the courage to leave a bad situation. It is so easy to settle when it comes to everything. As we get older, we either settle more easily or start to get a bit cranky about our precious lives. Settling leads to regrets; well-timed crankiness may get you a better life.

sex eight

Sex is all wrapped up in the specific, intricate, intimate story that shapes each individual. This is the inescapable fact that explains why sex can be so tricky and complex and wonderful and horrible and all shades in between. Oh my God, that other person can actually have a headache or not have a clue about their bodies or be utterly convinced that "Not tonight" means they are ugly.

It might not be a bad idea to listen to oft-repeated complaints, for clues to how to behave sexually.

1. Maybe most women don't like to be grabbed and fondled without warning. Every person feels like a subject in their own life, the star of the show. Nobody likes to feel like an object.

2. Maybe he means it when he says that such grabbing is a sign of his affection and desire for the woman.

3. Maybe men are built for almost as much sex as they can handle. Maybe women are too, if men would stop wrecking it by their grabbing.

4. Built into the complaint about "grabbing" are notable facts: women are far more turned on by a look, a quiet voice, and a slow, slow hand.

5. No means no. (If you need to say "No," you can say it with warmth and a promise, not as if you are rejecting arsenic.)

6. "No" does not automatically mean there is something wrong with you. Sometimes the other person really is exhausted.

7. Lots of kissing is a good idea, preceded by even more kindness and talking. Meanness, of all stripes, is a bad idea.

8. Adventure is exciting for the brain and the body. Mix things up. Surprise is the most powerful way to get attention. But please consider the psyche of the human being you are surprising. Consider how your actions will be received. And think about the

different reactions you might elicit: there is a fine line between surprise and shock.

9. Neither you or your partner are just a button to be pushed.

Christian Smith, a professor of sociology at Notre Dame, has done extensive research examining the lives of young adults. He notes that the combination of heavy drinking and unbounded sexual activity is threatening many lives and causing confusion and loss.

However, researchers found that the respondents seem to have a "tenacious, almost irrational desire to avoid regret" about their behavior.

I would argue that very few people are going to express deep-seated regret, shame and remorse at a first sitting with a research assistant. It took me four years of therapy before I saw "the worst thing about me" and another six months before I could tell my therapist about it.

It also might be too early for young adults to know the long term consequences of their choices. People can sure have regrets about not being careful sexually, for so many sad and tragic reasons, certainly as much as they may regret not sowing more wild oats. An "irrational desire to avoid regret" can lead to even more regret. It is too dangerous a world to systematically avoid warning signs.

Women used to be taught to save themselves for a man and then to "give themselves away." What I see as a therapist is that in the rough and tumble of life, very few women give themselves away to a man. It looks, instead, like we are all built to protect ourselves, be fiercely loyal to ourselves, even if the situation looks compliant and deferential. Often the apparent deference hides an inner caution or rage, a genuine and smart rebellion. The person we most give ourselves to is ourselves. Consequently, we are more self-protective in the bedroom than we like to think or advertise.

True intimacy is a lengthy, ongoing, back and forth process, filled with roadblocks and detours and clear sailing. Highs and lows abound in real sex. It takes about ten years to know another person and a lifetime to handle the emotional demands of intimacy. We may think we are "giving ourselves away," but that is probably shorthand for romantic fusion, tempting dependency, and loving idolatry of the other. When the other turns out to be disappointing or worse, our true self shows up in the anger, resentment and disappointment. The good news? We are built to love, not give ourselves away. We are built to have a loving time, not disappear in suffering.

chapter nine money

money one

A few facts can help:

It can be very hard to make money.

It can be very easy to spend money.

It is unfair and unkind that you do not get paid more money for the good work you do.

You may not need as much as you think you need.

You can figure out what you really want, what works for you. It might not be as expensive to live if you take the time to figure out what is really worth your hard earned money.

It took me years to figure out that a nice dinner at home can be as wonderful as a gourmet meal at a restaurant.

money **two**

I've been doing marriage therapy for over twenty years. I can count on one hand the number of couples who, as they fought about money, also had the facts in hand about the exact details of their financial situation. If you think your husband overspends, do you know how much he spends compared to what you spend? Have you agreed on a budget? Do you both track it?

It is so easy to have a free-for-all about money and let your partner have it. After all, it's easier to attack your spouse than your boss, far easier to fight about money than make it. And most of us would rather yell than be vulnerable: "I'm mad at you" is easier to say than "I'm frightened we're both going to go down with the ship." But it makes the long run a lot more difficult.

Perhaps you are scared about your money situation, so you do what comes naturally: you don't pay attention to it. This is the age old conundrum that is set in motion over many things. We avoid facing our problems and then our problems get bigger and seem way more insoluble. And the longer this goes on, the more impossible it all feels. Despair sets in. We feel different from everyone else, set apart, hopeless; defeated even before the facts are in. We feel like the only failure in town.

Facing things is a miraculous act. At first we are scared, but usually we loosen up as we see options and do something about the problem. We discover there are people who can help us. We discover we can help ourselves too.

People who do matter are starving and homeless. This is not a theory and a debate. It is not a dry statistic. People are in a lot of pain. Poverty is real.

Yes, we cannot fix everything. However, we can do something—for one person or one family in pain. If we have the wealth, we can do a lot more than that. The strategy is to move around all the noise, all the controversy, all our enfeebled feelings, and put a check in the mail or build a house with Habitat for Humanity.

It takes lots of practice, luck, wisdom, love and downright courage to square off with the complex reality of money. This will pay rich dividends. It is a rare and elegant life move to handle our money with dignity, daily awareness, and reverence. And we must ask, then, what would that look like in detail?

--We would pay attention to our overall money reality on a daily basis. It is not elegant to send out $700 worth of payments, while not knowing that we have only $500 in the bank. This kind of careless inattention causes a massive squeeze on the soul. Free-floating money anxiety is no joke.

--We would value our jobs and the worth we provide and endeavor to grow in self-respect and get paid what we deserve and need. We would treat others in the same way.

--We would save as much as we can, not only to be able to help others in need, but to help ourselves when the rainy day shows up, as it will.

--We would revere what our money buys—or not buy it if we can't revere it—because, again, everything that we spend our money on is provided by our own hard work.

To take money seriously is all about taking ourselves seriously. Both are way easier said than done. If we have managed money poorly for decades, we might feel hopeless about doing better. If we have only $500.00 in the bank, we might easily prefer to look the other way. Likewise, if we had a low paying job and no one really valued our services, it is next to impossible to have the self-confidence of a CEO. If we grew up in poverty of soul and possessions, it is not natural to take ourselves seriously, and so easy to undervalue everything we touch, including money and what we own.

It is easy to paint a picture of how we should live in any area of life. It is harder just to see what it takes to live that way, far harder yet to make it happen.

| money **six**

Applaud yourself for the money you do make. Do not be lackluster in appreciating what your partner does for you either, in terms of their financial contribution or any support they provide. Appreciate any effort that is made for mutual benefit.

money **seven**

My mother died when I was twenty. A few months after her death I was standing with my father at the back porch. He pointed to the skimpy drapes on the window and second-rate washer and dryer that took up little space. He said, "If I had to do it over again, I'd have listened to her complaints about those drapes and the cheap washer and dryer. If she was here now, I'd buy her good drapes and the best washer and dryer in town. Son, don't make the same mistake I did."

"The world is too much with us; late and soon

Getting and spending, we lay waste our powers"

--William Wordsworth

Getting and spending--we love it and so does Madison Avenue and our neighbors. It is good for the economy and our purchases reflect our passions, our necessities, our loves and our expertise. A mechanic buys tools, a reader buys books, and a scuba diver buys oxygen. We buy for our family, our friends, our charities, and for ourselves. A lot of this is elegant.

And yet I also wonder how much of our "getting and spending" is all about drifting. We buy more and more of something or everything because we haven't asked:

What do I really want?

What satisfies me?

Where is my expertise?

Where should my power be focused?

We are on our way to the mall. It's routine and normal. No one will notice that we have drifted from our heart's desire, our world class talent, the work that will make us money, or our health. We may prefer to not notice either, because the stuff that is really, really satisfying is scary and real and unique and individual.

If I am terrified to start my own company, I can just go drift on the hundred books I own on that topic. And when that fails me, I can just buy more.

194

chapter ten clutter

Untidiness, mess, disorder, jumble. This is the standard definition of clutter. It is accordingly a negative. Yet I wonder what the word is for the state of a room that evokes "cozy clutter"? Stacks of books. Lots of framed photos. Plants, decorative and possibly expensive "knick-knacks," open kitchen shelves filled with beautiful plates and bowls, piles of manuscripts on a desk, music books and handwritten scores on a piano. This is an active exuberant home-world, yes? A house that is hotel-neat or a kitchen that is organized like a hospital dispensary perhaps alerts us to a creatively deprived soul, a conversationalist of deadening predictability.

So--clutter is a personal affair. It is a matter of style. Whether it is oppressive or inviting to others may be a matter of degree, but it also definitely precludes very specific items. Cozy clutter would never include piles of unwashed sweaters or anything in cardboard boxes. Or piles of newspapers or anything else that is unattractive. It should never smother you or impede movement. It should only embrace.

Organization of possessions saves time, if we are talking about shoes, or keys. Being late for an appointment because you can't find something you need every day is not an elegant way to live. And yet, over-organization of almost everything else might prevent you from making accidental discoveries which could provide inspiration for new projects or new ways of thinking.

Clutter is a very personal, tricky affair. How does clutter effect your life? You already know something very important about you and "stuff" and elegance.

No big deal, perhaps, but answer these questions quickly:

a) What is your version of clutter?

b) Where is it?

c) How long has it been there?

d) What good does it do you?

e) What harm does clutter bring you?

f) Are you going to do much, if anything, about it?

Clutter is apparently a foggy, complex reality. You can be a hoarder and think everything is fine. You can get rid of things and miss them sooner or later. Ask someone close to you to talk about your clutter and their clutter. It could be a very interesting conversation.

clutter four

One of the reasons we have clutter in our lives is that we are not clear about what we really want to own or do. A master is first known by his limitations, yes, but what if we do not know what we want to master or who we really want to be? It is easier, less defined and less scary to be a generalist. It takes so little effort to buy one hundred things in the next few months. It takes a lot of effort to save a village in the next few months. It is easy to read The New Yorker every week. It is harder to read a scholarly publication and work towards the expert status you are seeking. Clutter covers fear. Clutter covers our vagueness.

It doesn't take a genius to know that the 130 tons of garbage taken from the home of Homer and Langley Collyer harmed their life in eviscerating fashion. We probably do not want 25,000 books, 14 pianos, pickled human organs or rusty bed springs in our homes.

Our "clutter" probably hurts us imperceptibly. An untouched piano. Unread books. Photos that haven't been looked at in thirty years. Files filled with totally finished business. It's only 420 pounds of neglected stuff, but it distracts us, mildly chides us, slightly wastes our energy, and doesn't make us feel lean, focused, tight and lithe. Clutter dullness. Clutter fatigue. Almost imperceptible in its hurt. So close to imperceptible that it is so easy to do nothing about it.

You know the Pareto Principle, the 80/20 rule. If you have 100 books, you use 20 of them 80% of the time and 80 of them 20% of the time. If you have 100 tools, you use 20 of them 80% of the time and 80 of them 20% of the time. Though I guess it would be harsh to say that 80% of those tools and books are clutter, one can harshly say that they hide the books and tools we truly value and need.

Clutter hides our gems.

I recently told a friend about the Pareto Principle. He laughed in appreciation of its insight and said "I think it is more like 90/10."

We each should have our cabinets and shelves and walls and (possibly) rooms reserved for our most sacred and revered things. We should set them apart from the fray.

And what should we do with the 1% of books and tools and poems and quotations and photographs and paintings that are our priceless treasures? Do you hang your Mona Lisa just anywhere? Do you put a pile of magazines anywhere near a book of Billy Collins' poems? Is this modern sacrilege?

Clutter can blind us to what really matters to us.

I am prepared to admit that this may be crazy, but I think the undisclosed purpose of clutter is to help us avoid the obvious limitations of our lives. If I keep everything as if it all matters, if I keep everything as if I can handle it all, then I am not admitting choice, limits, quality, judgment and finitude. Clutter keeps us blurred and foggy as we make our own Tower of Babel--the pile of books, magazines, emails, projects, duties and wishes that we will surely attend to, once we get our act together.

Clutter can be a sign of grandiosity. The pile looks like we think that we are going to live forever.

Maybe another undisclosed purpose of clutter is to hide our guilt or mask how difficult it is to accurately assess true, deserved guilt. Let's say you are buried in emails or feeling guilty about the latest novels you should have already read. You will then not notice that you have not returned five important phone calls. It will also be very easy to forget the poor and the downtrodden. Plus, with such a backlog to go through, there is no time to figure out your priorities.

Clutter makes everything look equal, either equally important or equally unimportant. I am convinced that clutter is an expression of our lack of fiercely defined individuality—as in "I want this" or "I will do this" or "I won't stand for this" which means "I do not want those twelve thousand things" and "I will answer those five calls" and "I'm here to save ten children from the world-wide sex trade."

Clutter is a distraction from our callings.

clutter **nine**

You can clutter your life with unending obligation to others, instead of learning to say "No" and having more time for yourself alone.

If we never forgive ourselves, if we never forgive others, if we do not work through our anger and disappointments and regrets, then we will be filled with emotional clutter that has accumulated for years. This inner turmoil will take a toll on our bodies, on our day to day clarity, and the way in which we deal with people in the present moment.

chapter eleven peace

| peace one

Keep your life at a do-able level, and stretch yourself step by step. Growing is an organic process, not a grandiose leap from an unsatisfied superego.

As you go about your daily life, why don't you feel great peace? Are you planning a massacre or something? If you are doing no harm, why don't you feel the blessed shalom? We all know why, no shame on you here. This is a scary world. Anxiety is a sane response to a scary world. And our monkey minds are brimming with guilt, comparisons, and the burdens of all we have yet to accomplish. Not to mention you may have been raised in waves of fear and recrimination and criticism—"the fathers have eaten sour grapes, and the children's teeth are set on edge."

No wonder some people go to church just so they can hear someone say to them "The peace of the Lord be with you." We all desperately need to do something about this peace gathering business, and I suggest you do truly see your good intentions, notice your no harm policy, and square off daily with monkey mind and remind monkey what Arlin Roy told me ("The superego is the devil") which means that we pay too much attention to all that negative courtroom business in our brain and nowhere near enough attention to our talents, our loving ways, and our good willed effort to haul ourselves out of bed every day and make the world a bit of a better place with the bit we do.

peace **three**

The 6 o'clock news is basically an orgy of brutality as mind numbing tragedies are slammed into our fragile minds and tender hearts. It does not foster compassion. It fosters disconnection. It is too much for us. We are out of our minds that we can even watch it one time, let alone most of our waking days.

Adults laugh about three times a day on average. Children laugh about three hundred times a day.

Healthy guilt is very specific. And it is part of a conversation, the long moral discourses of civilization, the detailed talk between you and the person you think you offended or who might have offended you. Healthy guilt is not a monologue.

"Chronic remorse, as all the moralists are agreed, is a most undesirable sentiment. If you have behaved badly, repent, make what amends you can and address yourself to the task of behaving better next time. On no account brood over your wrongdoing. Rolling in the muck is not the best way of getting clean."
-Aldous Huxley

Of course, the additional truth is that the muck is rolling around inside us and seems to have a life and power of its own. Sometimes the muck is what we have been told that we are—"You are bad," "You are a sinner," "You are spoiled," "You are a slut," "You are a loser." These messages not only drown out other voices, they ensure that other voices are not heard in the first place. You do not even know that you are being poisoned. Until at last, miraculously, something or someone tells us with such power and such steady insistence that the programming we have been subject to is wrong--and we begin to let in the light. The light of our innocence. The light of our goodness. The light of a new day. And we begin to exist in clean, fresh water and we can't believe our eyes, our bodies and our souls.

peace **seven**

We all live in our own separate movie. The movie playing in your head is only playing in the cinema of your brain. And my movie is only playing between my ears. We meet in the lobby to compare notes. It takes great skill and time to figure out another person's reality. Talk is essential, kind words, soft gestures, words of peace. "Oh, you are not mad at me?" "Oh, you like me?" "Oh, you really like me?" "You mean there is nothing wrong!"

peace eight

If you want more peace, go for more walks.

If you need convincing, listen to science:

a) Simple exposure to natural light stimulates healthy hormone production, which helps you feel better.

b) Walking stimulates healthful elimination of toxins from your skin and digestive tract.

c) Spending time in the presence of nature offers perspective and usually lack of chemical exposure, and gets you away from electronic stimuli and the accompanying unhealthy frequencies.

If you need more convincing, recall that a legion of great thinkers and writers and activists have attributed a lot of their genius and creativity to walking.

The more you walk, the more you crave to walk. As the body moves, the brain calms, and we may discover options in the largesse of the universe. In time we walk and live more lightly. We may even argue less, admit our errors more easily, and see our own bigger picture.

For those of you who are physically unable to walk, moving in any way will bring similar results.

The rest of us are urged to use that most miraculous of gifts: self-motility.

Peace comes like a gentle dove when someone whispers "No, sweetie, you've got it all wrong, nobody thinks that way about you, of all people." Or peace comes in the thunder of some friend who is sick of our darkness and wants to shout it out of us—"You are deluded, only you think that way--no one in their right mind thinks you are bad." Maybe peace comes from a long term therapist, who we know is truth-telling to a fault, and though this man or woman knows the worst about us, we are slowly, gradually changed by the unending respect and attentiveness.

What occurs in all these venues is a different perspective that lights up some dark corner of our life with a totally new reframing. We are all sunk in what therapists call ego syntonic pathology, where our pathology has become one with our ego and we see and feel no way out. The dissonant moment comes along as we reveal our guilt and shame or fear and someone truly understands, but differs wholeheartedly and significantly and steadily and wildly with our foregone conclusions.

As David Foster Wallace wrote, "We are all in a prison so complete that we don't even know we are in prison." We need others to open the door and tell us the unbelievable truth.

How strange to think that those who most differ with us might be the ones to save us and give us peace. But how do we recognize the truth? Next time someone differs with your perspective, especially one you have held closely for too long to remember, PAY ATTENTION! They may be wrong, but oh my dears, STOP AND THINK! Think of the possibilities, if they are right!"

No one is alert, assertive and present all the time. We can't help but daydream, fiddle around, and watch YouTube some of the time. We sleep--by itself the most vital component to what psychologists call "regression in the service of the ego." Sometimes we have to drift in order that our egos can be healthy. Sometimes the ship has to be back at port, or on dry dock. Every human needs a Sabbath, one drifting, playful day a week. Every soul needs fifteen minutes or more of silence or meditation or musing a day.

peace eleven

It is so hard to change. Here is one big reason why. You are like a ship that is adrift on the ocean of life. You have to fix the ship while it is still at sea. You have to do it while you are steering the boat. The ocean of life brings its own dangers to the ship. The currents pull us, the days go by fast, and it is impossible to notice everything, even harder to do everything. We drift partly because, at times, it is all too much. We drift because, sometimes, we catch a glimpse of the mystery and complexity of us, and it is all too much--so we stand at the ship's rail and gaze off into space. Eventually, we come back to the task at hand, and hopefully not too much time has passed.

peace twelve

"Joy is peace dancing. Peace is joy at rest."

--Frederick Meyer

peace thirteen

Slow down, when you can. Take it easy. Easy does it.

Now is the land of play.

peace fourteen

Do you remember what you used to do before the worries came? When there were no bills to speak of, no haunting fears about the significance of your legacy? What did you do, then? Did you go swimming in a lake on a blue sky day? Go to the movies or play chess or kiss your love for a long, long time? Did you listen to your favorite songs, over and over again? Reclaim these treasures with a vengeance and you will reclaim a treasured part of yourself and find more peace.

peace **fifteen**

A very talented, accomplished friend of mine lies awake at night, staring at the ceiling, as his superego (the part of our psyche that contains our critical conscience) goes over the failings of the day and once again makes things up, yet is convincing, haunting, and relentless. I said to my friend, "You should put a neon sign on your bedroom ceiling that reads My Superego is stupid."

Even my friend's neon sign would have to be supplemented with a thorough examination of his psyche and many ensuing talks. Nevertheless, all of us would do well to consider the possibility that our superegos may be archaic and primitive and sadistic and quite blind to the beauty of our achievements this very day.

chapter twelve reverence

Reverence. What emotion or image does that word convey to you? People moving slowly in a dark chapel. An Anglican chaplain walking by a stone wall in the English countryside. An audience laying flowers at the feet of a great dancer. Parents bathing a new born baby. A visit to the person who bathed you as a baby.

The word "reverence" is made up of the word "revere." To revere is "to regard with deference and devotion."

And so this question: what do you revere?

And another question: who do you revere?

When you revere something or someone, you are paying careful attention to that someone or something and you feel good in that presence. You are fully present to what you revere. You feel a sense of the sacred. And you are grateful.

reverence **two**

Start and end the day with a small ceremony to mark its adventuresome possibility and its quiet close.

226 | reverence **three**

Who reveres you? We all tend to look down the road for a huge fan club. Don't miss the people who already think you are special. Revere them.

The only vision I ever had occurred in Denny Lower's room in McGinnis House, a freshman dorm on the campus of Gordon College, Wenham, Massachusetts, USA. I lived there in a room next to Denny Lower, who was the RA (resident assistant) for the dorm.

It was mid-October 1972 and I was a freshman befuddled by the anxiety and depression and PTSD that comes from leaving home and entering a world five hundred miles away where no one knows you and no one seems to care. I was scared and sleeping through all this miasma, so much so that I had already missed a hefty amount of the required chapels and Denny Lower had posted a note on my door saying that he wanted to talk to me about me and chapel attendance sometime soon, like this afternoon at 3 p.m.

This note sent me into full blown paranoia and by noon my fantasies had me packing up my bags and heading 500 miles north back to Mommy and Daddy and a warehouse job and the long Canadian winter. There would be no need to announce my homecoming—the red face and smell of shame would precede me up the coast of Maine and suffice as advance warning.

Somehow, I managed to make it the ten feet across the hall to Denny's room and I knocked on what was for me the sure and certain door to judgment, purgatory and hell.

Abandon all hope....

Denny opened the door and asked me to sit on

his bed while he finished a letter that he had been working on. I sat on his bed and felt like crying, but back then (since I did not know meditation or deep breathing or negotiation techniques) I operated as far from my heart as I could with a LOGIC ZONE surrounded by 10,000 bricks that kept me and the dangerous others about 10,000 miles from my heart.

Being in the logic zone, I decided to play it cool and look around. And that's when the vision started. I looked at his bed, his chair, his clothes, the rug on the floor, the little art stuff on the wall—and I noticed that, though Denny was not rich, everything in the room was lovely and seemed to be hand-picked and arranged with care and elegance. It was like a little sanctuary of quality.

By this time, the room itself seemed to be filled with a white glow, which of course was either the color of my fear or the fact that it was a beautiful, sunny blue sky day and the brightness of the day was filling the room.

Then I looked at Denny and I saw him writing his letter and I noticed the way he held his pen, held the letter, and put the letter in the envelope—he looked like he was writing to the President of the United States. He was altogether focused on what he was doing and the way he worked seemed to match the quality of the room. His every move seemed elegant, rich, and full of meaning and significance.

He turned to speak to me and, right away, he put my fears to rest. "Bob, the Dean of the Chapel let me know that you've been missing some chapels and I told him that was no problem because as soon as I spoke to you you'd be making up for past mistakes. Is that not right?"

I eagerly shook my logical head with a resounding

"Yes" and even my heart, so protected by bricks and distance, could be found rejoicing and my face added to the glow of the room with a white relief.

Denny then said, "But that isn't really why I wanted to talk to you today." I silently nodded my head with a casual curiosity so Denny wouldn't notice that my guilt-ridden and fear filled heart was now dancing with the news that there was never any intention to send me to judgment, purgatory and hell.

Imagine the room getting whiter and the bricks melting and the logic zone dissipating when Denny looked at me and said, "You remind me of me when I was in college. A Professor at Wheaton College named Dr. Clyde Kilby took me aside one day and told me that I had a natural ability to really ask what life was about and see the preciousness of people and the wonder of existence. You are like that too, Bob, and it is a gift that makes you more special than you know you are."

I should have wept with relief. I should have grabbed his knees and hugged him as if he were the Prodigal Son's father. Instead, I discussed the theory of what he was talking about and played it cool—because you never know how vulnerable you look and how out of control you might feel if all the bricks get dismantled on one bright, visionary day.

But I left that room with the beginning of a vision— not really about me, but about how one can live: The way that Denny lived. I saw him for almost a whole year and everything he said or did was lived with the same kind of meaning, purpose, reverence, care, quality and elegance that was embodied in that room.

The vision I saw in him that day is a vision of the sacred, a sense that life can be a sacred journey. The enemies of such sacredness---busyness, rush, clutter and the like--all lie to us that life is elsewhere and tomorrow. This sacred attention does not scream out its beauty like a hawker at the Circus. But it can be very evident and very beautiful even in a small room as a man writes a letter and tells a scared young boy that grace is not only given, but it is within.

Our parents tell us to "Watch our drinking" or "Save 10% of our money;" our clergy tell us to "Honor the Sabbath and take a day off a week;" a friend tells us we're gaining "a little weight;" our partners tell us "Our temper is hurting them"...and oh the misery that would have been saved, along with the money, if only we had listened.

We end up saying "Yadda yadda yadda" to almost everything because we can never imagine that wisdom and revelation is here and now coming from the lips of an old man with a moustache or a friendly uncle or our parents (God forbid) or our local rabbi—no, we picture that our life-saving "truth" is coming in a FED EX box wrapped in royal purple from the palace in Dharmsala, India where the Dali Lama lives.

And so we miss the quiet fact that, most of the time (by far), the truth comes with a whisper, dressed in ordinary clothes, telling us something again, again and again—until finally we hear it or, because of repetition, the truth goes away and becomes silent and we hear only the usual chatter in our brains while we wait for the royal purple package to arrive.

How rare and wise to make the most out of every suggestion, every bit of advice and every word of wisdom that comes our way and to revere what is presently in our lives, as if buried within the people and the places we haunt is divinity itself.

It is natural for people to like us and even love us. If you think back to your younger years, you can remember the neighbors who really liked you, the aunt who thought you were special, the teachers who saw your gift, and the wonderful ones who wanted to kiss you. I've met very few who ever let that all soak in. It's not too late. Go sit by your back porch and let it soak in. The dazzling beauty of your humanity is evident from you and people saw it. They still do. Soak it in.

Have you ever noticed that the significance of anything human or earthly can be changed by the way we think or feel about it?

A cat can soothe your broken heart and the very same cat can drive a neighbor crazy. The person you love may be hated by someone else and the person you hate is somebody's baby. Your dream is compelling and has all your attention—but it will not make the six o'clock news since it does not involve murder, mayhem or ruin. Is a leaf falling from a tree worth our notice, does it matter if Australia falls off the map? Does it really matter if you fall off the map?

I would like to propose to you the intriguing idea that healthy spirituality, worthy of our humanity, is the disposition to love things and people in such a way that we make them bigger and better by our faith in them. And faith is our creative ability to see things as lovely, as important, as having far more potential than we usually think.

For some of us, it may be difficult to think about faith in this way because the topic is surrounded by loony-tune imaginings, religious wars, ignorant know-it-all people, and a thousand obscure arguments.

Or maybe someone, in the guise of the faithful, has scarred your soul deeply. If the latter is your case, you have my deepest sympathy that someone took what could be lovely and beneficial (faith) and turned it into an instrument of oppression, harm and abuse. Quite likely, faith's comfort may never be heard by you, and a forthcoming touch of grace will be anticipated as the grip of an enemy.

It may be helpful for you to forget the word "faith" altogether and substitute notions like big love, creative challenge, potential imagining, and attentive expansion. Or it may be helpful to tell you about my view of God, with the proviso that you understand I was once a serious philosophy student and find it very difficult to believe in anything. Philosophy rips everything to shreds. I once seriously doubted my existence, but that is another story.

I believe that God is the Big, big love that allows us to be, that allows us to live in this tapestry of beauty and pain where we can play and struggle and think and grow and, above all, see that there is more to that bird, that rose, that person, and that country than we ever knew. God gives us the more that allows us to be creators and makers of more—and the freedom that also allows us to sit and do nothing and to even make misery. And so in our terrible freedom we can drown the cat, blow up Australia, and cheer when you fall off the map.

Good faith is the viewpoint that we contain multitudes and that nothing is small, though we can make it small. Faith is possibility, glory unseen and now glimpsed in the very road we are on.

I have to tell you that when it comes to faith, and most things human, I believe in whispers and those who whisper. A woman tells me in a hush that when she was a little girl abandoned by everybody she prayed for God to show up for her and that night an angel appeared in her bedroom and told her everything would be alright—and it is the hush in her voice more than anything that has me listening, that has me convinced that there is more going on that meets the skeptical eye. A teenager tries you sorely and then one day you see her playing the piano with a soft touch and a gentle hand and the whisper of promise takes your breath away. A man cries over the woman who has broken his heart and you hear his cracked, hoarse voice whisper his pain and you suddenly see the staggering depths of both his humanity and the rules of love that need to be revered. It might be enough to make you think that Divinity made that man and those rules—and that it is not all an accident, a tale told by an idiot.

And yet all of this can be so easily dismissed—"the woman is a nut, the teenager is still impossible and the man is feeling sorry for himself"—or even missed altogether as we shout and rush amidst these quiet movements of grace. It is hard to hear a whisper in our noisy world.

I believe that faith is hearing those whispers-- whether it be in our praise of life's goodness, or in our lament at its brokenness and misery. And I believe, most of all, that the very best thing we can do for each other is to make more of each other and more of everything. An angel is supposedly seen. A piano is played. A man cries and the depth of the rules is noted. We can make much of all this or we can make little of it all. To me, faith is about making more and that is my whisper to you.

I offer you this excerpt from an essay written in 1953, which looks at a way of living as an act of faith.

"I believe that we learn by practice. Whether it means to learn to dance by practicing dancing or to learn to live by practicing living, the principles are the same. In each, it is the performance of a dedicated precise set of acts, physical or intellectual, from which comes shape of achievement, a sense of one's being, a satisfaction of spirit. One becomes, in some area, an athlete of God.

Practice means to perform, over and over again in the face of all obstacles, some act of vision, of faith, of desire. Practice is a means of inviting the perfection desired."

From "An Athlete of God," by dancer and choreographer Martha Graham

This piece was written at a particularly difficult time in my life, and I chose to leave in the sense of struggle and fatigue that life's difficulties can evoke.

I have yearned this past while to speak a few more words about healthy faith and I have not known what to say. Tonight I think I know. But first I want to whisper something about us. Has anyone told us lately that it is very, very hard to be a human being? Come here with me for a moment and rest in that truth. Just for a moment, let's drop our pretenses and our images and our facades.

The world is a tough, tough place.

It is very hard to be what we want to be.

Rest in that, take it easy, breathe, take a moment before it all starts up again, it will be alright, it is alright—not alright in the sense that everything is fine, but alright in the sense that you and I are fighting to make it better and though we fumble that is forgiveable too because we are all fumblers.

And so relax. Easy, easy, easy. Cry, if you need to. Your softness will do you mighty good.

Don't perform, you don't have to. We're just glad you are alive. That's quite the feat.

I have thought a lot about healthy faith, thought about this for my whole life. And tonight I can only say this. We are all too human and we cry and we are tired and we are very tired and yet there are gems that keep coming to me and I hope and know that there are gems that keep coming to you and it is those that keep us going, that fill our empty minds and empty hearts; it is those that make our lives shine—whether the gem be a lifeline of wisdom or a friend showing up unexpectedly or a child breaking the dullness with the sound of his voice.

A gem found me tonight. I was going to give up on all this for the tenth night in a row and a sweet friend sent me this out of the blue:

"I am reading "The Lost Art Of Gratitude" by Alexander McCall Smith. I am sending you a passage from it. There are good words preceding it but I'm too tired to type the whole thing."

(Two characters had been revealing their thoughts about God.)

"And there's Mozart."

She encouraged him to explain.

"Mozart, you see," he said, "is so perfect. If there can be music like that, it must be tied in some way to something outside us--it has to be. Some combination of harmony and shape that has nothing to do with us--it's just there. Maybe God's something to do with that. Something to do with beauty."

"Something to do with beauty. Yes, she thought, that was one way of

expressing it. Moral beauty existed as clearly as any other form of beauty and perhaps that was where we would find the God who was so vividly, and sometimes bizarrely, described in our noisy religious explanations. It was an intriguing thought, as it meant that a concert could be a spiritual experience, a secular painting a religious icon, a beguiling face a passing angel."

Can I whisper to you, without insult, that we are empty, we are very empty indeed? We, most of us, are starved for affirmation and love because most of us grew up in long silences surrounded by lots of criticism or worse. And we are starved because God does not fill us like a drug. We have to work to find God and that is good because we have to work hard to find most great things. But the great things find us too and that for me is my whisper of faith. The great things find us too. The gems. The wisdom. The friends. The voice of a child. Mozart. A concert. A beguiling face.

And it's only a whisper. Because tonight I'm tired and I'm vulnerable and I don't have all the answers. I just want to be quiet with you and tell you there is a depth to things that we forget, there is a depth to you, there is music to hear that is richly beautiful, there are sights for our eyes to behold that will renew us, and so pay attention and listen and stop and slow down and whisper to me something that is quiet and true and sacred and whisper what you know for sure and what has ravished you lately and who you love and what do you stand for and what has touched you with grace and beauty and hope. And you can cry and tell me where you have gone wrong and where you have been fooled and we shall tonight admit our folly and yet I will tell you that if you give us a chance we will see your beauty anyway and we will love you and you can rest in that love, a quiet love, a non-bravado love that knows you are tired and you are a mess too and the world is tough and it is hard right now as it has always been hard but the great things find us and we keep going and we shall be gems, we shall be gems (because we are all gems) and it is my whispering hope that God will find us too and we will most likely find God when we are soft and quiet and vulnerable, as I am now as I send you this.

At a case conference some years ago, one of my psychotherapy colleagues made this profound statement: "When you grow up in a really abusive home, what you are learning deep in your bones is that life is always elsewhere." We are given a script during our early years and we don't even know there's a movie being made. We learn a language created by the directors (usually Mommy and Daddy) defining who we are, and in abusive homes it can sound like this: "You're stupid;" "You'll never amount to much;" "You're ugly;" "You're bad;" "It's all your fault." What colors the movie even more is the atmosphere on the set that is way beyond words, of a family saturated with guilt or shame or hatred or despair. Long after you leave such a home, the movie plays on inside your head. You have learned that all the good things are not at your street address: life is always elsewhere.

Quite the poison, huh? Now mix that with two other things, advertising and familiarity, and let's see what a misery-making concoction we've come up with. Advertising is the medium whereby you learn that you absolutely need the new Lexus. Familiarity is the phenomenon wherein we get so used to the new Lexus that we will soon be looking for the new Benz to make us feel important and cool and significant.

In short, life is always somewhere over the rainbow and, after a while, we barely look up to see the rainbow because "it's just another rainbow."

What hope is there for any of us to be content and present in our lives, especially if you grew up in the kind of home they write books about? In fact, being present in your life is exactly the thing that won't happen, because you are always looking down the road to get to an "elsewhere" that will somehow magically transform your life. And if that place ever shows up, you will be subject to the Groucho Marx rule: "I can't respect a club that will have me as a member."

You will feel that your presence taints almost everything that shows up in your life and you will under-value so many things because they are associated with you. In your opinion, the "cool" people (whoever they are) will have better friends, sexier partners, attend finer colleges, have more illustrious careers, snazzier cars, and better homes and gardens—and jealousy and envy will become your intimate companions.

If you look at the Seven Deadly Sins, they almost all carry within them the latent notion that life is elsewhere: greed, lust, gluttony, anger, envy are all about more and "I don't have gold in my hand" and sloth is the despairing "Why bother?" that knows you are never going to get the gold.

I know this is all quite dismaying, but it can increase our empathy for one another and increase our understanding of why so many people are hooked by alcohol and drugs and chocolate and anger and yachts and orgasms and fame—because these have the temporary "juice" to make people feel something amidst their despair.

What can be done about this sorry state of affairs as we battle the overt and subtle poison called "elsewhere"?

The function of psychotherapy is to let you know that the movie that plays in your head is most certainly only playing in your head—and you are invited to other cinemas. Reality is the grand multiplex with endless movies playing and all of them are saying "You have not seen everything and there is something you don't know, especially about you."

The function of wise discernment and dialogue (in books, magazines, conversations, sermons, seminars, music and art) is to point out the poison of elsewhere and to pull us into the present with the disposition that beauty of all sorts and even the Divine can be found in more places than the front seat of a Lexus—and may even be found in you, of all places.

Gratitude is the sign that we've seen other movies and that we are beginning to know that we are not what we were told in the original movie. Of course anger will often precede gratitude in our journey towards perspective, as we are angry at the misery inflicted on us or (far harder to sustain) angry on behalf of others. Anger is the great clue that we want better for ourselves and others—doing something productive with our anger is the path to better.

A friend tells me that at a church on Cape Cod the service always ends with this benediction: "The only thing is love, everything else is advertising." Love is the cure for elsewhere: to love this good and present moment if it is good; to love your angry, hopeful wish for a better tomorrow; to let the love in that wants to adore you until you can eventually adore yourself; and to love others because their journey has probably been far harder than you can imagine—because even the person in the new Lexus might think he or she should be elsewhere.

I remember officiating at a wedding many years ago. It was an ecumenical wedding between a Christian man and a Jewish woman and I was asked to pick out something to read that was non-sectarian. I chose this lovely poem by Yeats, which I think he wrote for his own daughter's wedding:

> Had I the heavens' embroidered cloths,
>
> Enwrought with golden and silver light,
>
> The blue and the dim and the dark cloths
>
> Of night and light and the half-light,
>
> I would spread the cloths under your feet:
>
> But I, being poor, have only my dreams;
>
> I have spread my dreams under your feet;
>
> Tread softly because you tread on my dreams.

During my reading of the poem, the bride started crying and gently wiped the tears away from her face. Afterwards I asked her what had so moved her and she looked at me and said "When I was a little girl, nine years old, that was my favorite poem. I did not know who wrote it and eventually I forgot all about the poem. Until today, when you read it at my wedding. I can't believe it."

And she cried some more.

Oh, some days I think the softness is in charge and is going to win.

Over twenty years ago, a young man came to see me for therapy when I was in training at a Post Graduate school and Clinic in New York City. The man was tall, well-dressed, strikingly good looking, soft-spoken, and very nervous. He explained to me that he was a devout Christian but knew from early puberty that he was homosexual. He talked about his struggles to ignore it, deny it, and fight it. My mind started spinning all the theories that my training had given me about homosexuality, as well as the ways in which Christians are taught to view this orientation. I asked him what it was like for him emotionally to deal with his dilemma, and he told me something that took me far from theories and viewpoints. He took me from my mind to my heart, from theory to a person.

He said, "Ever since I was twelve years old I have gotten down on my knees every night by my bed and I have prayed this prayer: "Lord Jesus, change me by the morning or kill me in the night."

He was the first homosexual to come to me for psychotherapy. I have never forgotten him. You won't forget him either, will you?

I hope that in the days ahead I will be so rested, so clear-headed, so organized, so present that whenever someone talks to me and shares a dream, a pain, or a precious thought that I will be totally attuned to their unfathomable worth, their precious existence, and the beauty of this moment between us, which will never be repeated.

I hope that in the days ahead I will be so rested, so clear-headed, so organized, so present that I will make a difference when hardness has harmed that soft, tender soul whose life is real, who has a name.

And I hope I will be so rested, so clear-headed, so organized, so present that whenever I have a dream, a pain, or a precious thought that I will be totally attuned to my worth, my precious existence, and the beauty of my moment, which will never be repeated.

How elegant to live this way, an impossible ideal, but a far more wonderful habit than blindness to the glory that surrounds us.

Emotional elegance involves the deepest parts of your soul and how you live in answer to the following questions:

What is sacred for you?

What are your most cherished sacred experiences?

What are your most sacred treasured objects?

What have you always lived for?

What would you die for?

What is sacred is unique to every person. It could be your marriage, your kids, or waking up to see every sunrise. Sacredness, elegance--it's all very individual.

Can you imagine that every person in the world is as important as you and me? The starving father in Africa. The sex traffic slave in Asia. The Secret Service agent who lately blew it all for one night of over-rated folly. His humiliated wife. Can you softly and tenderly hold the realness of their lives in your hands and feel their hunger, hopelessness, fear, and shame? Can you see, with your soft eyes, that they are not stereotypes and headlines? Hey, that's Hamish in Kenya, Busaya from Thailand, and Sam from Georgia and his wife Tricia crying her heart out, all with one life to live, all tortured by the hard evils of the big world and the hard deluding evil within, and the pain we give to others and the pain we give to ourselves.

And what difference would this kind of impossible thinking make? Oh, this softness will not change everything. We know that, we know that deep in our despair filled bones. And yet softness changes things, one moment at a time, one person at a time, one crusade at a time. Softness keeps us from hardness. And if we are soft we will cry more, pray more, hold one another tighter, work harder and softer, and perhaps hope for a Big Soft Love that will one day banish all the hardness that hurts every very real person.

Traditional religious people have often thought of banishing evil people and the Devil and every manner of hardheartedness all to hell. Hell is an ancient way of taking evil seriously, hopefully in the name of love and softness and ultimate deference to goodness.

Hell is Big Soft Love's way of protecting softness. And yet I love the idea of Jesus descending into Hell, still banging away at the hardness, trying to soften up people so they can stand Heaven and see and taste its allure. The allure of softness and love and everyone is real and everything is divine. All things shall be well, and all manner of things shall be well.

All this is rather strange to the modern imagination and it is rather big and apocalyptic and most people who write about apocalyptic things seem to smack their lips in hardened glee over the victory of their side against the vast others who do not agree with them. And so it's the usual us vs. them with God on my side, not yours. It seems that St. Paul is the only believer who ever offered to give up his salvation for the sake of those people who, in his eyes, might not make it. He was a softie at heart. I can show you chapter and verse.

I certainly believe in evil and see more of its reality every week than most people. A psychotherapy career takes away naiveté and liberal foolishness, unless you are very asleep in your chair. Nevertheless, I wish for a soft apocalypse that will save everyone, a Second Coming where the angels are singing "Softly and Tenderly" and "Amazing Grace" and "He's Got the Whole World in His Hands" while Big Soft Love wipes the tear from every eye. And I close with the softest words of all, said, unimaginably so, from a very hard place by another softie: "Father, forgive them, they know not what they do."

We must keep working and hoping. It can all be better than it is, way better. None of this is easy. Negativity and doomsday pronouncements and cynicism are all too easy and add to our despair. The airways are filled with such cheap talk that costs its brayers nothing--for their noise does not lend a hand, wipe a brow, or pay a bill. Cheap talk is the noise of nothingness in the carnival of despair.

Dare you admit, in all your delicious softness, that you still have that secret dream, that ideal view of how you want to live? If you are approaching middle-age and beyond, you feel the tattered rags of your life. You are at the age where amazing grace is a necessity.

Grace is that soft loving sunshine that sees your beauty when you walk in the room, tattered rags and all. Grace looks beyond our flaws and failures and gently beckons us to still clean up our act and bring our dreams, our best self to the world.

Grace is softly beckoning you, still.

ferocity one

Some may say "I'm not fierce, I'm never fierce." Oh yeah. You eat every day and that is a fierce act. You bite and chew and are part of a process that agrees to kill things so that you can survive. You are ferocious.

And yet here is why you need to be even more ferocious.

We fight fierce things—and their fierceness derives from their speed and their invisibility.

Your book of poems will not be erased by an editor's hand. It will be erased by the invisible hand of fear.

Your clean closet will stay messy because despair will instantly overwhelm you.

Your yoga supple body will be delayed another year because procrastination will take you down easier roads.

You must become a master of ferocity. Here is a simple mighty act. Go to your calendar and block out one hour every day to do the thing you most want to do. Your book of poems. The Yoga work. The organizing of an elegant home.

One hour every day. It will kill one hour of TV or aimless surfing of the web or sitting in your chair dazed and defeated. You will shove fear and despair aside and bypass instant gratification. You will take a bite out of procrastination's thieving hand. And you will go to bed with the smile of a warrior.

It is very easy to drift with the tides of life, to succumb to the pull of flickering interests and insistent demands. The drifting state is often preceded by tiredness, numbness, indecision and too many options. We pull away from presence and let the tide carry us.

The fancy word for drifting is "passivity" which I've heard described as non-problem solving. The opposite of drifting is assertiveness. Assertiveness is the engine of every action. Eating is assertive, writing a letter is assertive, deciding to do anything is assertive. To stop doing something is assertive. Good news, therefore: you are more assertive than you think.

Most of us tend to notice the areas where we are not assertive. We idolize the more aggressive types (the CEO's of the world) or only notice extreme aggression. We fail to see the thousand ways we are assertive--in our endurance, patience, forgiveness, and starting over for the thousandth time.

Drifting is not easy to stop because we can be so used to a zoned-out state that we may not even notice we are in it. We may drift out of habit. We may drift when we are scared, overwhelmed, confused or sad. Or maybe we have never sat down with ourselves long enough to know where we want to go and want we want to do.

And therein lies the best recipe to counteract drifting: have a picture of what we want our inner and outer life to look like. If we know what we are trying to do this week or month or year, it is easier to see if we are getting anywhere. And if we share our plans with an assertive guide, that person can be our look-out, too.

There are phrases parlayed about that blind us to the inner mechanics of our soul. "What are you holding on to?" is one of them. "Just let it go" is another.

In truth, we are not holding on to anything. Nor do we just let things go.

For example, you may be "holding on" to too many books and you need to let them go. Or so they say. Here's the real deal. As you grew up, you did not believe that you were the source of all knowledge and excitement or the original fountain of self-confidence. And so you bought books in order to learn, lose yourself in an adventure story (or find yourself), and you bolstered your self-confidence by surrounding yourself with books. Cool.

You did this thousands of times and so, over time, books and you became inextricably bound. They are now holding on to you in your unconscious, and possibly in every nook and cranny of your house, with more on the way. These books mean way more than a non-book reader could ever imagine. If you are told to "let them go" or stop holding on to your books, you are being told something that misses the profound, steel-like grip that books have in your life. It misses your ferocious love affair with books.

If books and you are going to part company, it would take thousands of moments to convince you that you need or want them no more.

We hold a pillow to our chest or a cup in our hand. We let go of the cup as we set it down. Easy. This is not the same as the hold that we have with books or food or money. Nor is it the same as letting go of hatred, lust, revenge or anger. To let go of this stuff is hard. It requires a lot of soul work and heavy duty equipment to cut through the steel cables that bind us to what we have become and what we have done, possibly for decades. If a man has lusted after women for decades, he is not going to be chaste on a Friday night.

I give you permission to be the King or Queen of your empire, since this is already true. So, dress up, speak up, issue some royal decrees, and take a magisterial role over all your domain. And do not abdicate your throne to mild ducks like passivity, drifting, numbness and detachment. Practice royal living in every moment, attend to detail, pay attention, add dignity and planning and appropriate power to each thought and each motive and each action. A King is always a King, a Queen is always a Queen--there is no room for slackers in your palace. Mediocrity does not befit your importance. Ascend.

A therapist was counseling a beautiful woman and her fiancé. The woman confessed that she thought she was very ugly, despite all the protests of many people in her life throughout the years. The therapist listened for a bit and then he grabbed her by the arm and told them both to follow him as he rushed to a nearby bathroom. He got them both to look in the mirror and he asked the woman what she saw. She said "I see an ugly woman." He asked her fiancé what he saw and he said "I see a beautiful woman, a loving woman with a very pretty face, a very lovely body." The therapist told the woman to look into her fiancé's eyes and to see in his eyes the truth that she might never see for herself, but could learn to see through his eyes. The therapist said, "You are never to look at yourself through your eyes, only through the eyes of your beloved. And I mean never."

It is perhaps the rushing to the bathroom that is most telling in the therapist's exorcism of craziness, for the rushing contains his belief that one ought not to casually sit there and chat with darkness, which is itself a wild, pernicious and unruly foe. The rushing contains the secret to sanity, which is also wildness. We look at the world through the eyes of those who love us, we become wild enough to hear the "never" and listen to it and follow it, and we never ever dialogue with our craziness or stay in our bed when darkness has descended, and we run to the shower and get the juices flowing and we turn up the music on the stereo and we go over to a friend's house and we hear their love, feel their love and live off the crazy, wild notion that we are crazy and that others are sane who love us and tell us that we matter and then we go do wild things like feed the hungry or write a poem or go to an AA meeting or do our best at our jobs, and this is all wild because it is the creation of what wasn't there before, a band of brothers, a band of sisters, lighting up the candles that miraculously make all the difference in the world.

Perhaps the chief sign of neglect in someone's life is a leftover feeling of dullness and insignificance—a sort of "Oh well, what does it matter?" at the center of a soul.

How can we live with more passion, competence, and care if we have been treated with neglect and neglect ourselves in certain ways?

It is not easy, but these ideas can help.

The moment to be saved from neglect is right now, this can't wait a minute longer. The truth is that if you have been treated with shabbiness of any sort, you have been treated with poison. But this poison does not come with a warning label—only with the certainty that you deserve such a poison because you are defective and you are not worthy. And this assurance tells you to put up with things because other people matter more. And it tells you not to make a fuss because "Who do you think you are?" and "Stop your complaining and don't be so self-centered."

This is all a lie. It is evil—and the sure sign of its evil power is that it kills dreams and passion and possibility with no sign of struggle or complaining. It all seems like a natural process---"Oh well, what does it matter?"

Some people have stood up for you, they have told you that you matter and that you can live better and that you deserve better.

You must listen to them and stop the habitual ways you will easily brush off their warnings, their affirmation, their love.

This is not easy. Neglect is easy. This is a lot of work. Neglect is not a lot of work. This requires faith amidst great doubt. Neglect requires nothing. You must fight the evil of neglect with the ferocious intention that your life deserves.

And so right now you must listen to some music, some music that touches you and inspires you and makes you feel like there is possibility for you and a new passion within you. Do whatever gets you into your best space. And as you listen to that music, or go for that walk, or pray, or meditate, you must remember the people who have not neglected you, who have cared-- indeed, who have loved you—and you must dwell on their love, for these are the angels of truth who have told you that you matter. And then you must find a sword—the sword of anger that will fight every lie and hate every moment of neglect that you have been given, the fierce sword of love that will put power and meaning and competence into every blessed thing you do. And you must kill the poison-filled thoughts that come automatically from your history, your depths, and the drenching wet rags of foolish neglect. And you must create, in a thousand different ways, the atmosphere of dignity and quality and aliveness that the angels of love have wished for you with all their might.

think **one**

Thinking, contemplation and diagnosis are essential to a life of emotional elegance.

Thinking is work.

It takes time.

It can be painful.

But you can't get to where you want to be tomorrow if you don't know where you are today.

Thinking is essential stress.

Who validates your life on a daily basis?

Who says what matters and who matters?

Who has taught you to value certain things and to think that other things are not worth the time of day?

Who has shaped you?

We are all deeply shaped by our families and friends, our peers, our teachers, and our total environment. But, eventually and ultimately, we each need to be the authority on our own success. This is a crucial aspect of being successful—being your own authority, living by your own standards, and having the courage to shape your own life.

think **three**

Think about....

1. The people you love the most.

2. The people who love you.

3. The things you like to do.

4. The ways in which you are competent.

5. Your biggest achievements.

6. The top values that you live by: (no, you don't have to be perfect in following them, but you really do endorse that everyone should live this way.)

7. The loveliest thing you own.

8. Your favorite room.

9. Your favorite place on earth.

What are your emotional strengths and weaknesses? Emotional burdens and complexities? What gets to you and makes you depressed, angry, despairing? What makes you feel ecstatic? What is it like to be you on the inside?

You might be prone to anxiety about money or despair about your sexual life. Or maybe you are ashamed of your body or arrogant when it comes to political viewpoints.

What emotional pattern would you most like to enhance in the days ahead?

What emotional pattern would you most like to defeat?

Here is a diagnostic questionnaire that asks you to say a word or two about certain important emotional realities that help or hinder you.

In the following areas, rate your life as objectively as you can on the scale from -10 to +10 with zero being a neutral mid-point between the two extremes of -10 representing "This area of my life is a total mess and causes me massive despair" and +10 being "This area of my life is a total success and causes me great joy, happiness and well-being". For example, you might rate your ability to handle criticism as a -2 because every critique feels like an internal earthquake, and yet in terms of gratitude you are a +8 because you consistently see the lemon becoming the lemonade.

If you prefer, write a word or two, or a paragraph, about any applicable item.

GRATITUDE:

POSITIVE THINKING:

ENDURANCE:

COURAGE:

REALITY-ORIENTED:

RECEIVING COMPLIMENTS:

ENVY/JEALOUSY:

ANGER:

DRUGS:

FEAR:

GUILT:

SELF-CENTERED:

SHAME:

SADISTIC:

MASOCHISTIC:

APOLOGETIC:

DEPRESSED:

SELF-CONTROL:

ANXIOUS:

PROCRASTINATION:

LAZY:

SMALL-MINDED:

PASSIVE:

OPEN-MINDED:

CLOSED-MINDED:

GROWING:

ALCOHOL:

FAITH:

NOTE: If you want to grow, be brave and share your reflections with someone who really knows you and see what they have to say. We are all blind to our own blindness and an outsider can help us see what we do not see.

Take a look at your current life, and think about everything tangible that you would like to get in order. What is on your back? What needs to be eliminated? What do you have to square off with? What is getting to you in terms of your surroundings? What needs done?

This can be simple things like painting a shed or cleaning up your desk. It's all about your unique life. Trust me when I tell you that getting things done is indispensable to elegant living. Everything that is not the way we want, drags us down.

This is fairly obvious, but somehow we might not make time to do these types of things. We may view them as inferior or secondary or not very significant in the big scheme of things. We might not be skilled at painting the shed or have the money to hire a painter. Or we might resent the time it takes to do these "dumb" things. However, creating what we desire will give us peace and self-respect on all levels.

What comes to mind as you think about the following aspects of your life? If a certain category does not apply to you, just move on to the next one.

Myself

Partner

Son

Daughter

Step Son

Step Daughter

Grandchildren

Father

Mother

274

Brother

Sister

Aunt

Uncle

Grandfather

Grandmother

Grandfather

Grandmother

Friends

House

Hallway

Kitchen

Dining Room

Living Room

Bathroom

Bedroom

Study/Office

Garage

Yard

Job

My Body

Money

Compassionate Outreach/Charity

Political Involvement

Reading

Exercise

Hobbies

Sex

God

My Past

The Future

think **eight**

What is the biggest thing you would like to stop doing?

What is the biggest dream you would like to accomplish?

What questions do you have?

Do you hear the questions and then rush off to somewhere else?

Have you already heard the answers, from within yourself or from someone else?

Do you hear the answers and then rush off to somewhere else?

Are you ready to do the work hidden or revealed in the questions?

Are you ready to do the work hidden or revealed in the answers?

To all who offer and receive advice, including me...

Has anybody hurt your feelings lately? If so, chances are it was because someone was giving you what they considered to be well meant advice.

Don't you hate it? Isn't it mind-boggling how hurt you can be? You seem to forget this, and then someone gets to you, often someone close to you, important to you. And you are suddenly in so much pain. It hurts so bad you'd think it was the first time your feelings ever got hurt.

You feel like a big toddler. (Shhh....we don't want the word to get out.)

You try to be logical about it. You know that you need advice, feedback, and criticism. You know that no one succeeds as a salesperson, a spouse, a parent, a student or in virtually any human endeavor without the flow of giving and receiving advice.

Yet you also feel, feel, feel and live this heart-soaked truth: You hurt. You want to run. You worry that you can't hang in there like you know you are supposed to.

Advice often hurts, especially unsolicited advice, which is the kind we most often deeply resent.

Advice hurts because we are tender people. And once we are hurt, we are left reeling, confused, perhaps angry and ashamed. We wonder if other people feel so easily bruised. We wonder if we are wimps if we don't express anger at how the advice was given. Should we show any feelings at all? Do we always have to appear totally together if we are going to make it in the rough and tough business world?

How many times have you been present when someone got their head handed to them on a silver platter and everyone in the room knew that something wrong had just happened but everyone kept their mouth shut, especially the guy with his head on the platter?

And we've all heard the true stories of someone like Steve Jobs, founder of Apple, with all his wealth and all his brilliance, using his power to crush some undeserving soul who has made the mistake of not being perfect while working against impossible deadlines and exacting judgment.

We feel so powerless.

To make matters worse, there is a poison in the air that affects us all.

I would bet a small fortune that someone has hurt you lately and then invited you to not take it personally. I would bet another small fortune that when you told others about the incident that they invited you to "let it go" and to move on. Or you were told to not let anything get to you in the first place.

And I would bet further that you felt alone, misunderstood, and very tempted to go live on a desert island.

Don't go... not just yet.

Let's examine this advice you are given about advice, and see if it holds up as you read about two of my psychotherapy clients who began the long process of teaching me that people are not healed by this cheap advice, a hug, one intervention, a sharp rebuke, or the newest fad or miracle to come down the pike. They gave me permission to tell their stories, but I changed the details to protect their identities.

I warn you that this is not pleasant reading, and you can skip this italicized section if you so desire.

P. had sex with her mother at her mother's command from the age of five to forty seven. If she did not comply with her mother's wishes, she was told and thoroughly believed that she was BAD, BAD, BAD. As she got older, and even while she was married, this daughter thought it was her absolute duty to still have sex with her mother....after which she was told that she was evil and therefore appropriately punished with cigarette burns on her body. I won't say where. The daughter had no doubt that this was right and she felt horrific guilt if she did not love her mother in this fashion.

P. stopped therapy before she stopped having sex with her mother, so I do not know what became of her.

"What if we are locked in a prison so complete that we don't even know we are in prison." (David Foster Wallace)

When I met J. she was twenty years old and had never been on a date. She was in so much emotional pain that, just for distraction, she would cut her arm, pour ammonia on the cut, and light her arm on fire. And that pain was less than her emotional pain. She would come to therapy and was so scared of my rejection that she would not talk for at least the first forty three minutes of a forty five minute session.

She worked seventy hours for seventy dollars at her local Catholic church. A Catholic priest was the first person to have sex with her-but don't be outraged, he cared for her and the love did her good. At home, she lived in her own apartment, above a mother from Hell who beat her almost every day of her childhood years; and then, among other things, she was forced to cut up her own poop when she was a teenager.

J was in constant agony, and that agony included waking up in the middle of the night absolutely convinced that there were burglars in the house. She would patrol her house for an hour and a half of utter terror and then go back to bed. This meant her life was one of perpetual fatigue. As someone once said, tiredness is the cousin of depression.

All the time, her skin felt like there were bugs crawling inside it. All the time, her brain was absolutely convinced that she was "stupid, stupid, stupid." J knew with complete conviction that she was a complete loser in every way.

Eventually, after years of hard work in therapy, J. left the Church work and got a job in a local government position. She has had two good boyfriends, makes decent money, sleeps through the night, and no longer cuts and burns herself!

When we read stories like this, we should know in our bones that **a lot of the advice we are given about success and failure and dealing with criticism is quietly pernicious, grossly inaccurate about human experience, and impossible to follow.**

Here is a litany of what we are being told:

"Accept responsibility for everything that happens to you."

"Don't take anything personally."

"Just let it go."

"Move on."

"Don't let it get to you."

"People set up their own pain."

"People want their pain."

"You are poor (or fill in the blanks of whatever is wrong with you) because you want to be."

"Time heals all wounds."

Now think of your hurts, your fears, and the tragedies that have accompanied your journey.

And think of the people who live in North Korea, many who are literally born in their underground prison systems and have no idea they are in prison; think of a teenager growing up in the violence of Syria; think of a person born with a low I.Q; think of the above women whose story I shared...

And here is what I propose as a serum to the poison that saturates our culture. This is a Manifesto about Advice:

1. We are responsible for some things in our lives. We are not responsible for other things. It can take a lifetime to figure out the difference.

2. We can't "just" let go of massive hurt. There can be no limit on grief; forgiveness is a long journey when someone shot your son. The same with "move on." It can take months to pack up your possessions and move to the West Coast. Far harder to understand that the furniture in your soul (low self-esteem, bitterness, fear) is bolted down. Internal pain and brokenness go with you, even if you go out the back door and never return.

3. Things either get to you or they don't. You don't "let" them get to you. If someone meets you for the first time, shakes your hand, and says "My, you are ugly," that is going to get to you, because that person moved past your defenses before you even had a chance to know what a jerk you were dealing with. The next time you would have to be on guard.

4. A knife to the stomach will hurt even if the attacker did not know you personally. An insult can hurt your feelings even if the insulting person is just having a bad day and claims to not mean it personally. To respond to criticism and attack requires enormous practice, a shrewd and strong ego, autonomy--and even then, people can get past our defenses with their creative and surprising sadism.

5. Sometimes people do create their own pain, though I do not like the words "set up pain." When you rob a bank, you always think you're going to get away with it. The old saying: "One hundred things can go wrong when you are committing a crime; you're a genius if you can think of ten of them." The same with drinking too much, eating unhealthy food, cheating on your taxes--you feel the instant

gratification and forget about the hangover, the far off diabetes, and the knock on the door from an IRS agent a year after you filed your tax return.

6. I do not think that people want their pain. I think they want the pleasure associated with the pain. A man too afraid to look for a better job is scared. It's not that he wants or likes poverty. People don't want to be broke. Yes, they may not want to work or might be lazy, but I'm sure they'd accept the winning Lottery ticket or five million dollars from you.

7. Time does not heal all wounds. If you doubt me, ask a doctor or peer into your own soul.

The problem with the poisons we breathe is that it all **blames victims**, whether it is you, who were left speechless by a sadistic attack disguised as advice, or the crushed people who put one foot in front of the other and walk into my psychotherapy office.

I repeat: we know we need advice. We admire those who have pointed out our faults and we became the better for it. We admire our heroes who have listened to advice and had the brains, guts and tenacity to learn, to grow, to reach the top, to put themselves out there, and to push past their fear and insecurities. We know that money matters immensely, that people have to work hard to climb the ladder of success, and that many people prefer excuses, alibis and blaming others to facing their fears and heading in a better direction.

We know that people can be given too much empathy, empty assurances, and false hope. Edwin Friedman, the marriage and family systems therapist, woke therapists to the fact that too much empathy can, indeed, defeat therapy in that the purpose of therapy is to help people grow, not to receive sympathy forever for a terrible childhood.

Still, bad advice is bad advice. And good advice poorly given does not help us tender people receive it, and we need all the help we can get.

This holds true even if, or perhaps especially, the advice takes place in a religious context.

Let me show you what I mean, and I can best do it by being a bit more personal and telling you another story:

I happen to be a Christian, though I do not believe easily. And I hear so much evil every week that I wonder if God is a very absent help in trouble, just like the writers of the Bible seemed often to lament. Nevertheless, I still have faith in Jesus and hope that one day "All things shall be well and all manner of things shall be well." (Julian of Norwich)

The blaming of victims is particularly galling to me when it comes from Christians because they do not mirror the exquisite sensitivity of Jesus, about whom it was said *"A bruised reed he will not break, a flickering candle he will not quench."*

I have a client named Cathy who gave me permission to tell her story. In the course of her marriage, she had a miscarriage early in her pregnancy. She lost another baby in the seventh month of a second pregnancy. Her step-daughter committed suicide in a psychiatric hospital. And, about five years ago, her eighteen year old biological daughter died of a heroin overdose.

It is maddening to realize how many Christian books and websites only make her feel worse about the tragedies she has experienced or the darkness she battles on a daily basis. In more ways than one, she has been told that God won't give her more than she can bear and that heaven will make these tragedies seem like incidents in the light of eternity. She has been indirectly accused of holding on to her pain through bitterness or not letting go of fear which is viewed by many as a self-imposed prison. The truth is far uglier. Fear is almost always created by difficult people and hurtful or evil circumstances. It is the prison we are often thrown into, before we are even able to spell the word "fear." Or it is the abyss which consumes us as we feel how scary life can be.

The last thing people need when they are beset by unimaginable pain is a string of clichés, said so repeatedly, so thoughtlessly, so habitually in a misguided effort to help. Silence is far better, or a hug, a tear. This will diminish the domino effect of insensitivity that hurts people so unwittingly.

I believe that the hoped for reality of heaven, which Christians speak about, will wipe away tears from every face, finally mend the broken, and that eternal love will make up for the enormous evil of the world. To paraphrase the agnostic philosopher, R.W. Hepburn, the Gospel is a symphony of restoration and salvation, and any other proposal that does not offer life after death is a flute solo of comfort by comparison. And yet the comfort of the Gospel has to be delivered in the tone of the Gospel which is "Rejoice with those who rejoice and weep with those who weep."

Every Christian who talks or writes about these things should read C.S. Lewis' "A Grief Observed," Nicholas Wolterstoff's "Lament for a Son," or Frederick Buechner's "Telling the Truth: The Gospel as Tragedy, Fairy Tale and Comedy" in order to see how believers can acknowledge tragedy as tragedy, write about it with sensitivity, and still embrace faith, ragged though it might be. Or, far better, perhaps every Christian should read Ecclesiastes before they write or say anything about faith:

> *I have seen something else under the sun:*
>
> *The race is not to the swift*
> *or the battle to the strong,*
> *nor does food come to the wise*
> *or wealth to the brilliant*
> *or favor to the learned;*
> *but time and chance happen to them*
> *all.*

This, from the Bible, is a far cry from the glib *"Everything happens for a reason."*

Even St. Paul said *"We were so utterly unbearably crushed that we despaired of life itself."* Maybe God won't give us more than we can bear, but life sure will, even if you are an Apostle.

Thirty years ago I thoroughly believed that people could be healed by a hug or one therapy session. I used to argue with my teachers in therapy school that therapy was a rip off because it took too long to fix people. And then I became a therapist and listened to people in whose shoes I could not walk ten feet, let alone a mile. These people are not healed by one session or a thousand sessions, though they want to be. Nor are they healed by well-meant religious or spiritual or Christian advice, even though it sounds triumphant and compelling.

Bad advice is still bad advice.

When I was a teenager, before I was ever kissed by a girl, I was convinced that sex would fix everything. I don't even believe that one any longer.

The only thing that fixes everything is, well, everything. We need love, mental health, fit bodies, community, money, good work, friends, family, rest, healthy spirituality, and a just and peaceful world, among other things. We need far more than "Just let it go."

The best preparation against the inevitable hurtful advice we are going to receive is to build a life that we are proud of, so we are less defensive and reactive and can recover faster from the inept and clueless comments that come our way.

The best preparation against any of us perpetrating such nonsense is to walk a mile in another person's shoes.

If we do not understand the internal damage done to tender people, if we under-estimate the evil and injustice in this world, we will not muscle the energy, the justice, the wisdom, the patience, the action and the time that love demands that we give.

Your journey towards emotional elegance can be further shaped by reading. Here, with comments and a few quotations, is an ensemble of books, blogs, and websites that have brought riches to me.

David Allen's *Getting Things Done: The Art of Stress Free Productivity* is a book that I would claim as indispensable. The best introduction to GTD that I have read is "Organize Your Life" by James Fallows, Atlantic Magazine July/August 2004.

Frederick Buechner has been a friend since 1981 and he is a widely esteemed writer of spiritual truth. I especially recommend *The Sacred Journey*, *Eyes of the Heart*, and *Telling the Truth*. It was Buechner who pointed me to John Irving's *A Prayer for Owen Meany*, Mark Helprin's *A Soldier of the Great War*, and the Depford trilogy (*Fifth Business*, *World of Wonder* and *The Manticore* by the Canadian writer, Robertson Davies--all novels full of wisdom and idealism and mess and life and grace.

Father Robert Farrar Capon, Episcopal priest, theologian, New York Times best-selling author, gourmet cook. His book *Supper of the Lamb* is a masterpiece, a book unlike anything you have ever read. It is a cookbook that will lead you to think about life and onions and wine and tuxedos in a fresh new way.

Michael Dirda is a Pulitzer Prize winning book critic for "The Washington Post." His "*Book by Book: Notes on Reading and Life*" is a library of wisdom in itself. Here is one of my favorite quotations from the book:

"Where is your Self to be found? Always in the deepest enchantment that you have experienced." --Hugo Von Hofmannsthal

I discovered Balthasar Gracian's *The Art of Worldly Wisdom* in the early 80's, when it was out of print. Around election time, The New York Times ran a column in which thirty people were asked, "What should the next President read?" One of them chose this book, referring to it "as the wisest in Western civilization." I got a copy from my Seminary library and took over a dozen pages of notes. Shortly after the Times piece, the book was republished and has remained in print ever since.

James Gustafson *Self-Delight in a Harsh World* (W.W. Norton & Co. New York, NY. 1992) is the work of a psychiatrist who seems to have read everything and he offers deep perspectives from political theory, history, English literature, and his own field.

I acknowledge with gratitude the work of Dr. Kevin Hogan, persuasion expert, psychologist and marketing expert. His extensive research serves as an ongoing back-up to my work and writing as a psychotherapist.

Dr. Thomas Howard was The Professor of English when I attended Gordon College in Wenham, Mass. from 1972 to 1977. He was one of the most liked and well-known teachers, partly because he had written a couple of books that were beloved by Christian students looking for a way to love life and God at the same time. For this exact reason, his autobiography *Christ the Tiger* was a breath of fresh air for me. And his writings introduced me to the whole notion of sacred living. His second book, *The Antique Drum*, was a more theoretical paean--an argument against the 1970's emphasis on impulse, instant gratification, and disorder. A later book *Hallowed Be this House* is very germane for our purposes here, because Dr. Howard goes through every room of a house and looks at what goes on it that room from a spiritual perspective. His chapter on the bathroom talks, for example, about the need for cleansing and for privacy. This book is a unique gem.

I am grateful for all the works of C.S. Lewis. Who cannot be enchanted by *Narnia*, the space trilogy, *The Screwtape Letters*, *Surprised by Joy*, and Lewis's sheer breadth of learning? Who cannot be grateful for all that Lewis had a hand in and pointed to--*The Lord of The Rings*, the work of Charles Williams, and Dom Bede Griffith's *The Golden String*--the latter being the spiritual autobiography of one of his students.

I have enjoyed the poetry of Mary Oliver, whom I first met through her 2007 book of poems called Thirst and her oft-quoted words:

> *"Ten times a day something happens to me like this - some strengthening throb of amazement - some good sweet empathic ping and swell. This is the first, the wildest and the wisest thing I know: that the soul exists and is built entirely out of attentiveness."*

I became a minister when I was young. Twenty six years old. Ron Peck Sr. was one of the members of my church and he saw my youth, the complexities of the church, put two and two together and offered to "sort of watch your back," as he put it. He was forty-four years old and had a no-nonsense, "don't waste my time with foolishness of any sort" stance. He had filled his kingdom with a fine family, good friends, a beautiful home that he built himself, and a vision that life should not be small, though we are very prone to make it that way. I was glad he had my back, though it cost me a few stern warnings about some of my miscues and batches of ignorance.

You need someone in your life that will affirm you, guide you, and be like a lighthouse pointing the way--a lighthouse that won't budge about your folly.

Who is your Ron Peck?

The War of Art by Stephen Pressfield is a much heralded "vital kick in the ass" (Esquire magazine).

When I was a student at Princeton Theological Seminary, the brightest student I met there was a budding Jesuit named Gary Dorrien. Gary fell in love with a woman, left the Order and went on to be a successful theologian and brilliant scholar. Gary put me on to the best thing I read in Seminary, the two issue New Yorker profile of Walker Percy by Robert Coles. I stayed up till the early hours of the morning reading the profile when Gary lent me the magazine.

Walker Percy awoke me to the whole notion of "everydayness" and how we are conned by fashion and fame and familiarity to miss out on the splendor of our lives.

> *"The search is what anyone would undertake if he were not sunk in the everydayness of his own life. To become aware of the possibility of the search is to be onto something. Not to be onto something is to be*

in despair." (From his novel, The Moviegoer)

Women Food and God: An Unexpected Path to Almost Everything by Geneen Roth is a jewel of a book. It evokes holiness in the best sense of the word. Anne Lamott says: "This is a hugely important work, a life-changer, one that will free untold women from the tyranny of fear and hopelessness around their bodies. Beautifully written, a joy to read, rich in both revelation and great humor."

David Schnarch Constructing the Sexual Crucible: An Integration of Sex and Marriage Therapy (W.W. Norton & Co. 1991) is a mind-altering walk through the complexities of human emotion, behavior and thinking when it comes to relationships, sex and marriage. He warns us eloquently about the poison in many therapeutic viewpoints. He invites us to be adults.

Wilfrid Sheed In Love With Daylight: a Memoir of Recovery (Simon & Schuster, New York, NY. 1995) Mr. Sheed makes sobriety sound more appealing than any other writer I know. He is funny and wise.

Michael Bungay Stanier is a Life Coach from my home country of Canada. See his Find Your Great Work (Box of Crayon Press, Toronto, Canada 2008).

I add here a host of men and women whose Internet work are models of business acumen and emotional savvy: Ronna Detrick on feminine spirituality and deep conversation; Seth Godin on marketing; Molly Gordon at Authentic Promotion; Danielle LaPorte's The Fire-Starter Sessions; Mollie Marti of Best Life Design; Kate Swoboda on Life Coaching; Michelle Ward of When I Grow Up Clubhouse; Roy Williams, the Wizard of Ads, of The Monday Morning Memo; Samantha Bennett of TheOrganizedArtistCompany. com; Erika Lyremark of The Daily Whip; Brian Kurtz of Titans Marketing.

&

And I must mention Rumi, Rilke's *Letters to a Poet*, the chapter "Delight in Order" in *How To Do Things Right: The Revelations of a Fussy Man* by L. Rust Hills; Thomas Kelley *A Testament of Devotion*; Donald Hall *LifeWork*; Barbara Brown Taylor *Leaving Church: A Memoir of Faith*; "On Being a Self Forever" in *Self-Consciousness: Memoirs* by John Updike; Iris Murdoch's *The Sovereignty of Good*; the book on golf and spirituality called *Golf in the Kingdom* (now out as a movie); *Wind in the Willows, Harry Potter, The No. 1 Ladies' Detective Agency* series by Alexander McCall Smith; *Gilead* by Marilynne Robinson; Anne Lamott's *Bird by Bird*; *Tao te Ching* (translated by Stephen Mitchell); M. Scott Peck *The Road Less Travelled*--all of these, most elegant and poignant and unique. And there's more--& and & and &.

acknowledgements

I am deeply honored and grateful that David Allen wrote the preface to this book.

Many thanks to all those who read early drafts of this work and offered valuable comments: Katie Hogan, Arlin Roy, Carl Heick, Jim Beverley, Michelle McNeight, Laura Beverley, David Spagnolo, Aaron Beverley, Michael Milea, and the participants in The Emotional Elegance Club.

Marian Grudko deserves extra gratitude for her painstaking review of the whole manuscript. She is brilliant on a macro and micro level when it comes to editing. She can be reached at MarianGrudko@gmail.com

Some of this material was first published in "The Dig", my weekly e-zine that is hosted on my website www.findwisdomnow.com. The webmaster for this work is Vince Martinez of 123webconnect.com. Thanks, Vince, for your competence, warmth, integrity and impressive always-on-time efficiency.

This book and accompanying website was designed by Elliot Toman of asubtleweb.com. I am grateful to Elliot for his patience, warmth, and aesthetic gifts.

I cherish the community of family, friends, colleagues, ministers, therapists, authors and teachers who have shaped and supported my journey and offered me their varied elegance.

I am also grateful for my clients who have taught me so much about relationships and what works and what does not work in life.

Bob Beverley

300

Bob Beverley is a psychotherapist in the mid-Hudson valley of New York State, USA. He has written *Dear Tiger: A Book for Tiger Woods and for Us All*, *How to Be a Christian and Still Be Sane* and *The Secret Behind the Secret Law of Attraction* (with Kevin Hogan, Dave Lakhani, and Blair Warren). Bob is available for motiva-  tional speaking, consultation, and psychotherapy.

Bob is a native of New Brunswick, Canada. He graduated with a degree in philosophy and English Literature from Gordon College, Wenham, Mass. He spent a junior year abroad at the University of Edinburgh in Scotland. He received a Masters of Divinity from Princeton Theological Seminary. Bob received a Certificate in Psychotherapy and Marriage and Family Therapy from the Blanton-Peale Graduate Institute in New York City in 1991. To learn more about Bob Beverley, please visit his web site: www.findwisdomnow.com

302

Made in the USA
San Bernardino, CA
01 October 2016